W9-CFH-224

Will I ever forget this day?

Will I ever forget this day?

Excerpts from the Diaries of
Carol Lynn Pearson

Edited by Elouise M. Bell

Bookcraft

Salt Lake City, Utah

Library of Congress Catalog Card Number: 79-54897
ISBN 0-88494-390-9

First Printing, 1980

Lithographed in the United States of America
PUBLISHERS PRESS
Salt Lake City, Utah

The Diarist

She wrote words,
Addressed them to me,
Put them in a bottle
And sent them out to sea.

Time and the tide
Have brought them to my sand,
Continents away.
We stand strangers, she and I,
She of a different name.
Even our bodies are not the same.
(After seven years, I'm told,
Not one old cell remains.)
If we met on the street
I might not like her much.

I pick up the notes
And a voice — so young — emotes
Enthusiastically an endless stream
Of loves and fears and dreams.

She speaks even the words
That are not there,
The words between the lines,
"Know me — understand — care."

All that adolescent glory —
And the pain —
Mostly it was the pain,
I think, that did it.
You can't look that closely
At someone's pain
And go unmoved.
And her voice — so young.

I let fall the final note.
Her story, for the moment, ends.
Across the continents, we embrace,
Understood,
Forgiven,
Friends.

— Carol Lynn Pearson

Contents

How this book happened

Elouise M. Bell

A wise old Southern deaconess once said something important about a common human weakness: "Everybody wants to see Jesus, but nobody wants to die!"

All of us, at times, want to reap what we haven't sown. We want to be able to play a graceful Chopin prelude without putting in the hours of practice required. We love to get letters, but hate to write them. We enjoy reading other people's diaries, but somehow can't get around to keeping our own.

Which brings us to the story of how this book came to be.

Several years ago, when I was a member of the General Board of the Young Women (formerly MIA), President Spencer W. Kimball began urging young people to keep their own personal journals. Because the Lord had commanded us all to keep records, and because the prophet was emphasizing the commandment, journal-keeping was made an important part of the Young Women program. Church magazines carried good articles about record-keeping, and blank journals of all kinds appeared in the bookstores.

But — we all know how good intentions sometimes get lost. Hundreds of brand-new journals were lying around in the homes of the Saints, still waiting for that first (or perhaps second) entry. Countless young people sincerely *intended* to get going on their personal journals, but somehow just hadn't done so yet.

What to do?

Well, example is a great motivator. If young adults in the Church could *read* some journals, could see what other young Mormons wrote and how they went about it, perhaps that would help.

When I learned that Carol Lynn Pearson had kept a journal faithfully since her senior year in high school, I urged her to publish a book of excerpts as a means of motivating others. When I first made the suggestion to her, she laughed and dismissed the idea. (Read her introductory letter to find out why.) But after much soul-searching, Carol Lynn agreed that I could go through her diaries and choose excerpts, and then we would *consider* publishing a book.

So that's what we did. Excerpts were chosen for one of two reasons:

1

1. Because they were interesting in and of themselves.
2. Because they revealed something significant about the art of journal-keeping.

Every now and then, I added an editorial comment of my own on the subject of journal-keeping. These comments (set in italics) usually deal with specific questions and problems, and are offered as suggestions to help stimulate the reader's thinking.

As you read these journal samples, remember that they are just that — excerpts, bits and pieces. The actual diaries contain twenty times as much material. The excerpt printed here for any given day may be only a small part of what Carol Lynn actually wrote on that date. I have tried to include enough of the journal entries so that you can follow the thread of what's going on and so you can also see a variety of the things she was interested in; even so, there will naturally be many gaps.

The further I read in her journals, the more convinced I became that Carol Lynn's diaries would be excellent for the purpose we had in mind. For one thing, she had been (and still is!) a marvelously faithful diarist. Through all the nine years covered here (from her senior year in high school to her European travels and then her job as scriptwriter for the Brigham Young University Motion Picture Studio), Carol Lynn made entries every night, with *very* few exceptions.

Another reason I thought Carol Lynn's diaries would be a good choice is that so many people identify with her. Again and again, people respond to her poetry and plays by saying, "That's just how *I* feel!" or "That's just what *I* would like to do!" As a young college student, she was in many ways a typical Mormon girl: she came from a family of modest means, sewed or saved up to have the clothes she wanted, put herself through college on scholarships, and worried about the same things that most of us worry about during those years.

In fact, the three central concerns recurring in her diaries are ones that most committed Latter-day Saint youth have. You may want to follow these threads through the diaries, so let's identify them here.

First, Carol Lynn was deeply concerned about her relationship with the Lord. This was a central priority. Time and again, she raises questions in her journal about what the Lord wanted her to do, or how he would feel about a certain course of action.

Second, she wanted to know what it meant to be a woman, and what part love played in a woman's life. Her quest for these answers was sometimes hectic, sometimes sad, sometimes funny — in short, typical of the human condition.

Third, she searched diligently to know how best to use her talents. Perhaps her skills in acting and in writing were exceptional, but the *problem* remains universal: every young person has the responsibility of identifying talents and putting them to best use — in other words, becoming a wise steward.

Perhaps all this talk of journals has raised a question in your mind: just *why* are we commanded to keep journals? It's worth thinking about.

What value does a personal record have to the person who keeps it?

More than anything else, a carefully kept journal serves to *testify* to the individual that the Lord loves and watches over him or her. One of the most dramatic accounts in the Bible tells of the Lord's deliverance of the children of Israel at the Red Sea. It was such a marvelous event that they never forgot it. Forever after that, when the Israelites became discouraged and downhearted, someone was sure to stand up and cry, "Remember the Red Sea!" The recorded account of the Lord's power and his love buoyed up their spirits during the dark days. Young Nephi used the very same story to give courage to his people (see 1 Nephi 17:26).

In just the same way, a person who has kept a comprehensive journal can look back through his own record on days when he needs courage and a boost to his faith and can read in his own words accounts of how the Lord has blessed him. That's why it's important to recognize spiritual experiences in our lives, and why it's equally important to record them.

In addition, keeping a day-to-day record causes a diarist to develop a sense of responsibility for that greatest of all gifts: life itself. When we keep an honest record, we don't need anyone else to judge us: we know whether we are making good use of our time and talents. If at the end of a day we can record worthwhile accomplishments and significant goals reached, the glow of satisfaction we feel is evidence enough of our diligence. On the other hand, if day after day we can fill the pages of our record with nothing but trivia, the verdict is equally clear. You will notice in Carol Lynn's diaries

3

how often her journal writing causes her to pause and reflect over the day, to wonder if she is doing the right thing, to make decisions to do better. A good journal is an excellent form of personal accountability.

Finally, a good journal is a record of our spiritual and emotional growth. That's one of the reasons it is so much fun to read back over your old journals, even just one year later. It's satisfying to see how far you've come, to realize that problems vexing you twelve months ago have been solved. A well-kept journal allows you to take satisfaction in your progress, or to make resolves and plans where progress hasn't been so great. As President Kimball says in his article on journal-keeping, "Your own journal, like most others, will tell of problems as old as the world and how you dealt with them" ("The Angels May Quote from It," *The New Era*, October 1975).

But what value has a journal to *others* who might read it? For that matter, should others read it at all? Many young people worry about others reading their diaries. After I had done most of the reading of Carol Lynn's journals and editing of the excerpts, I mentioned the project to several students. They immediately asked how I felt reading another's personal diaries — and how *she* felt, knowing I was reading them.

Well, for my part, since I was reading diaries kept during a period a number of years in the past, I felt that time had given a certain objectivity to what I was reading. All of us think, say, and do things that are pretty sensitive or "touchy" at the moment; with the passage of time, we are less embarrassed about them. In all honesty, I have to say that my reading of her journals only increased my respect and admiration for Carol Lynn.

But *why* read others' journals?

As in the case of the diarist himself, others find in journals a testimony of the Lord's dealings with his children. Abraham explains this in the Pearl of Great Price: "I shall endeavor to write some of these things upon this record *for the benefit of my posterity that shall come after me*" (Abraham 1:31; emphasis added). The same purpose was in the mind of Moroni when he wrote the title page of the Book of Mormon — a record made, he said, "To show unto the remnant of the House of Israel what great things the Lord hath done for their fathers."

Another value of a journal is the *insight* it gives about the writer. Sometimes the writer has become a public person, and his or her

4

early writings are important for the light they shed on the individual's development. Church leaders, civic and government officials, artists and writers, scientists and scholars — what influenced these people, what made them what they are? Early journals not only inform, but instruct and inspire. In the article mentioned previously, President Kimball explains that as we read the accounts of great men and women, "We discover that they did not become famous overnight, nor were they born professionals or skilled craftsmen. The story of how they became what they are may be helpful to us all." As just one example, countless thousands have taken courage and inspiration from the famous *Diary of Anne Frank.*

Even for those of us who never become famous, diaries serve as an important link between generations. A teenager reading her mother's early journals may gain insight and compassion she could not get any other way. Truly, journals turn the hearts of the children to the fathers. And, on a larger scale, they turn the hearts of human beings to one another across time and distance, for as we read personal, honest accounts of another person's life, we are struck with the reality of being brothers and sisters. No formal biography can bring us as close to someone as can that person's own journal, written in his or her own words. No legacy you may one day leave your children and grandchildren will have quite the impact your own record will have.

A third sometimes-overlooked value of journals to other readers is the great historical and sociological importance of these written records. Maybe it's hard for a fourteen-year-old girl to realize that the details of her daily life will one day be of interest to a sociologist, anthropologist, or historian. But first-hand accounts of how people lived and felt in any given culture are of great value in helping succeeding generations understand that culture. Decades from today, centuries from now, people will be interested in what kind of part-time work twentieth-century teenagers did, how they traveled to and from school, how they decorated their bedrooms, what kind of clothes they wore.

All these reasons — inspiration, insight, and information — explain why the Church Historian's Office asks people to send diaries and journals to that office for microfilming (originals are returned), and why the Brigham Young University Library has established a special Women's History Archives to collect diaries, letters, and pa-

5

pers of Mormon women. When the time comes to write the history of *this* period, such records — because they are primary, first-hand sources — will be invaluable.

To sum up, let me quote again from President Kimball's article. He wrote: "Get a notebook, my young folks, a journal that will last through all time.... Begin today and write in it your goings and comings, your deepest thoughts, your achievements and your failures, your associations and your triumphs, your impressions and your testimonies.... Maybe the angels may quote from it for eternity."

Carol Lynn Pearson

December 5, 1978

Dear Elouise,

I am reconsidering. I think perhaps I can swallow my pride and let you go ahead on the book. I feel so strongly about encouraging people to keep journals that perhaps I can beat down my innate modesty and my need to protect my image.

As I told you on the phone my reservations are these. It appears to me terribly egotistical for anybody who is not yet dead to offer their diaries to the public view. If we do the book, we will keep to the early stuff, and you must make it firmly known that this was *your* big idea, not mine, and that I consented under duress.

Just the fact that I have become somewhat well-known in Mormondom does not make the mundanities of my life any more significant than the mundanities of anybody else's life. I do not have the compelling circumstances of an Anne Frank to make my diaries immortal. In my mind I see an intelligent person picking up the book as she wanders through her local bookstore and saying: "My gosh, her diaries now. Who does she think she is?"

So here's who I think I am. I am someone who, from some fluke, has caught the attention of a lot of people who like to quote my poems and see my plays. But other than that my life is very much like theirs. I am one of them. Perhaps I could better convert our particular audience to journal-keeping than could a formidable figure who is removed from them. That is, if we do not bore them to death in the

6

process. Do you think we can find enough stuff that can keep them awake?

You asked me to write down some of the benefits I feel I have received from keeping journals for twenty-one years. Okay. Since we began talking about this project last spring I read through the entire body. What a profound experience. Even the boring parts interested me. You know how we're told that when we die our whole life will pass before us? To have that experience without the dying part is even better. As I sat in my chair and read, I saw twenty-one years of my daily actions, my thought processes, my growth, my dis-appointments, my stupidity, my wisdom, my ignorance, my fears, my exaggerations, and a bit of courage. Going through all that was an amazing, amazing experience. Nothing less than profound.

Here are some of the specific benefits I feel I have received:

I think I shall be much more sensitive to the growing pains of my own children. Reading through my adolescence was so embarrassing to me that I really think I'm better prepared to withhold judgment on someone else. Possibly, in some future crisis, I may let one of my children read a few tear-soaked pages of my own, showing them that everybody, even their very own mother, goes through that kind of thing. It may help them to appreciate my own humanity as well.

And even beyond my adolescence, it was the same thing. Some-thing happened to me that at that time was a Very Big Deal, and I recorded it as such. Looking back on it, I put my hands over my face and say, "Oh, please, my dear, spare us." It develops compassion. To the person who wrote that, it was a Very Big Deal. And the reader should muster a little reverence (as well as a knowing smile, of course).

Keeping a diary, I believe, forces you to be honest. Frequently in the reading I would find myself saying, "You're kidding. I said that? I did that? I felt that way?" Evidently I did. At least that is what was really going on to the best perception of the writer at the time. And that kind of Large Dose of Reality is helpful along the way, too — not just looking back on the long haul. I remember sometimes in my teenage years making a near-past event into something bigger than it really had been. Then in reading back a few months later I could put it in a little better perspective.

Another benefit to writing things down is simply that we forget so very much, and a small reminder can bring back a whole event, or

7

conversation, or feeling that otherwise would be totally lost. Frequently as I read I found myself shaking my head and saying, "I had completely, totally forgotten about that."

It has become something of a tradition in our house to use diaries on birthdays, both my diary and the children's. I find the pages that describe the birth of the child, and read them aloud. I think it gives a fine education on birth, as well as a sense of the child's origin and belonging. We then read from the diary that I have kept for that child, recapturing some of the highlight events and, of course, the marvelously funny things that child has said. They enjoy this very much.

Requiring ourselves to express verbally what we're experiencing helps us, I believe, to understand better those experiences. On December 20, 1960, I wrote: "I don't think that I could ever presume to be a great writer, but I love to write. I feel most truly that however much of my feelings I can transpose into thoughts and then into structured, legible form — so much of myself I am master of." I really believe this. It's easier to be sloppy about what we're thinking and feeling when we don't write it down. But when we require expression of those thoughts and feelings, we have to deal with them, look at them more carefully, see what they're all about. The result? We understand ourselves a little better.

Being able to document and observe the changes that have taken place inside of me has been tremendously interesting. I watched myself mellow considerably. In my youth I was such a smart alec. The conversation recorded in this entry was typical:

B: You have very nice hands. I didn't notice them before.

Me: Well, they were here.

Years later, I am still a smart alec. But I observe that with a little maturity warmth tempers wit, and I can feel that progress has been made.

Another development I enjoyed watching was my thinking on "the woman question," which has been a very pronounced theme in my life. To see the origins of my first observations and questionings and to watch the evolution of my philosophy helps me see the whole picture more clearly.

On the subject of what we write about other people in our journals, let me say that in general I do believe in expressing feelings honestly. How we react to others is a part of our lives and adds to the complete and final picture. I would be careful, however, of writing down what is simply gossip, or information that might come to us about others that is none of our business and of a highly personal nature. At the same time I must stress that I do not believe in "whitewashing." My own record will be a record of the bright side and the dark side of many people. For years a joke among my friends has been, "Watch out — Carol Lynn will put you in her diary for that."

Whenever some enthusiastic person asks me for advice on how to become a writer, I always include the suggestion to keep a consistent diary. The practice of putting your thoughts and observations down on paper leads to clearer thinking. The discipline of spending those moments in writing develops the discipline it takes finally to write a full-length play, or a novel, or a short story. And the things written down sometimes can be the source of future writing. For instance, my poem "Bethlehem" has as its very obvious source the description I wrote in my diary of the day I spent there.

A final benefit that I feel I have received from having kept all these diaries and having taken the time to read through them is an inescapable awareness of the ongoing movement of life. Nothing remains entirely constant. The good days are followed by the bad, and the bad days are followed by the good. Looking back over past anguishes that were absolutely crushing and then seeing the pages gradually let in the sun again gives me a more tangible hope that present and future anguishes are not as eternal as they seem in the darkest days. This is quite comforting.

A few miscellaneous suggestions to the beginning diarist: Do not stick to writing only events and not feelings. In my reading I frequently got bored with what I was doing back then, but never with what I was feeling. And in reading other diaries, such as some of the early pioneers', how often I found myself saying, "Okay, okay. So you spent the whole day sewing, or traveling, or attending the sick. What's going on inside of you?" Too often there are no indications.

Do not count on remembering the things that are so important to you at the time that you know you will never forget them. I come to an entry like, "Had a most significant talk with Larry." *Go on, go on!* I say to myself. But I didn't go on then, and I can't go on now. I would love to know the gist of that conversation. But it is gone forever.

Make an effort to write daily, but don't be discouraged when you miss. Here there is no gold star for perfect attendance. But hopefully you will get to feeling guilty if you miss too many days. Often have been the times when I had to put aside very high-priority work to

9

catch up on my journal. I was hooked, and I felt a strong compulsion to keep it going.

If the book you are considering writing in has just a few lines reserved for each day, forget it. A perfectly blank book is preferable, so you may write as much or as little as you need to and not feel you're messing up the structure. A hardback attractive book with lined paper is fun to write in, but less expensive notebooks will do just as well. The first nine years of my diaries are in a variety of hand-written books, a collection of seventeen volumes of all sizes and colors. I then decided in the interest of time I would type my entries. Consequently I have many hundreds of pages that I must soon divide into years or perhaps eras. Writing by hand definitely adds something of intimacy, but in my life just now it's typing or nothing.

Well, Elouise, I give you permission to do the book. Go ahead — ruin me — unveil me to all my fans as the melodramatic adolescent that I was (and maybe still am). I hope they will be charitable. If it causes some of them to more seriously consider keeping a written record of their own lives, then it will be worth it. For I know the benefits to them, as to me, will be invaluable. My last word to them is this:

Jan 25, 1961. Am I being presumptuous in the assumption that the events and thoughts of my life merit recording? No matter. I'm very important to me, and that's enough, I think.

Blessings on you. And me. And them.

Love,

Carol Lynn

1

"If only I could write on paper what I think in my mind..."

The year is 1956. Former General Dwight D. Eisenhower is the grinning, popular president of the United States; handsome, silver-haired David O. McKay is president and prophet of The Church of Jesus Christ of Latter-day Saints. In the small Mormon town of Provo, Utah, the tempo of life has picked up once again as thousands of college students return to Brigham Young University. Up and down tree-lined University Avenue, the leaves have started to change from green to gold and scarlet. Many tall trees shade the grounds of Brigham Young High School on University between Fifth and Sixth North. One of the students enjoying the excitement of being a senior this year is Carol Lynn Wright, who has just turned seventeen. Carol Lynn is slender and animated, with unusually large and expressive blue eyes; she is talented in acting, debate, public speaking, and writing. She lives half-a-dozen blocks from school, at 630 North 600 East. Regrettably, her home lacks the warmth, cohesiveness, and "heart" that most Mormon homes enjoy, for the mother has been dead two years. The family consists of the father, Lelland Wright; twin brothers Donald and David, age 20, who have just left for missions as this diary begins; brother Warren, 18; and sister Marie, 15. Relationships within the family, though amiable, are not close, and as a result, Carol Lynn's life focuses on school, especially extracurricular pursuits such as drama, debate, and the school newspaper; on church activities; and on her circle of friends.

Sep 26, 1956. Dear Diary: Since this is my last year of high school (quite unbelievable), I am going to keep a record of it. Today I was

11

elected editor-in-chief of the *Wildcat*. On Wednesday, I had an immense thrill! All on His own initiative, He came over and indulged in an hour-long, inspiring, educational, and uplifting conversation concerning everything from mashed potatoes to religion.

Oct 9, 1956. Well, tomorrow is Homecoming, and, just as I expected, no date.

Oct 10, 1956. Well, today is Homecoming, and I suppose the dance is just breaking up. I sort of wish I'd have gone with J., but I just didn't want to.

Oct 12, 1956. Today we (Mary Anne, Linda, and I) were in the Church Office Building, and we met this sweet little old man. He's done lots of work in the temples and knows many of the General Authorities. He took us around and we met some. We met Mark E. Petersen, Levi Edgar Young, and Patriarch Eldred G. Smith. They were all really wonderful. Mr. Bergen talked to us for a while, and we walked around the temple. I've never met anyone like him, and I'll never forget the things he told us.

But of course she did. Forget, that is. That's one of the first reasons for keeping a journal. Wouldn't you like to know what the interesting little old man told Carol Lynn? So would she!

Oct 15, 1956. I had an hour discussion with my "psychiatrist" today (Mr. Mink [*school counselor*], that is). We talked about polygamy and whether a person could love more than one mate. He didn't convince me, and I'm still rather upset about it, but I'll just remember what Mr. Bergen said, and wait and see. "Only he who made hearts can weld them together."

Oct 16, 1956. I sat and talked with Liane tonight for four and a half hours, supposedly creating for the paper. We discussed our distraught emotional lives and decided it was hopeless!

Oct 25, 1956. Our roadshow was tonight —"Red Wings" — and I've been in the tub an hour trying to get the Indian paint off.

Oct 28, 1956. I think I saw His car tonight, traversing the alleys and by-ways.

Oct 30, 1956. Today school was dismissed so we could go up and hear

President David O. McKay in Devotional. It was really very impressive and good.

How much does "impressive" tell us? Even a sentence or two summarizing President McKay's talk would have served to help recall later. The briefest quote will help you "file" talks and speeches in your mental cabinets so that you can retrieve them when you like – perhaps not in full, but in outline, at least.

Oct 31, 1956. Halloween. Today has been a *very* eventful day! Even more important than the fact that Britain bombed Egypt is the astounding news that I am making sure progress with Him!

Tonight we had our Thespian Halloween party. We were supposed to all dress up and give a little rendition from whatever we were. I went as Uncle Remus and put black gunk all over my face. I gave "How Br'er Rabbit Lost His Long, Bushy Tail." Anyway, He was there, and I could have died because I looked so haggy — like a true Halloween witch. After the party we decided to go downtown trick-or-treating. So we all piled into the cars and took off. Either by coincidence or clever scheming (mine, that is), I rode with Him, along with Mary Anne and Blaine. We went downtown and sang Christmas carols, did the bunny-hop down Center Street, and generally disturbed the peace. It was truly something to write in my diary about. I wonder if He will put it away in his files? Ah, well, 'twas beauteous!

Nov 9, 1956. Today I saw His coat, the one He wore Halloween night. It's got black all over the right shoulder. From me, no less. Now we're even; He left quite an imprint on me, too.

Nov 10, 1956. I will always remember this as the day I was disillusioned. When I read this in ten years, I may laugh at it. I hope so. But right now, I feel that either I am crazy or the whole world is wrong. I wish there were something else for girls to marry besides men. At this moment I have a very dim outlook on life, and it will take a drastic happening to change it.

It didn't take quite ten years to see this traumatic incident in a different light – see the entry for November 10, 1957. But chalk up another advantage for journals: going back even one year shows us how our ideas have changed, how we have matured, convinces us that we are progressing.

Nov 11, 1956. "Prepare for the worst, hope for the best, and take what comes." I'm just going to enjoy not having a crush on anybody.

Nov 12, 1956. I do think I will survive, but it will take time and heartache. In the meantime, I'll just be giddy and have faith.

Dec 13, 1956. If only I could write on paper what I think in my mind! I feel very much like those people who are suffering nervous breakdowns must feel.

Another reason for keeping a journal: so that some day, someone (perhaps a granddaughter or a niece, perhaps a total stranger) can read what we've written and exclaim, in relief, "I didn't know anybody else felt that way!"

Dec 31, 1956 - Jan 1, 1957. Well, it is now 1957. I tried to make some New Year's resolutions, but when I tried to list all the things that are wrong with me, I just can't take it. I often wonder *what I am.*

Jan 3, 1957. I discovered some old poems I'd written last year; they're very nostalgic.

Jan 5, 1957. I accomplished quite a bit today: housework, homework, and my Sunday School lesson.
   Yesterday, when I talked with Mr. Mink, my preference test showed that I'm most interested in the arts (writing, drama, music). That's fine with me!

Jan 15, 1957. Will wonders never cease! I actually won the poetry contest! Literally, I won first place in both serious and light verse, but I could only receive one first place, so in the humorous, I received second. Also, in the religious division, I won honorable mention (fourth place). All in all, I'm only thrilled to death; it was one of my lifelong ambitions.

Feb 8, 1957. I have the most horrible guilt complex about even applying for that leadership award. I feel like a first-class A number-one hypocrite. But maybe we appear worse in our own eyes than in others'. I hope so. In any event, today marks the arrival of a better me — one who might *deserve* a leadership award!

Here we see a journal not only as a record of growth, but as part of the motivation for it as well. Writing about her feelings of guilt made Carol Lynn

14

resolve to do better. And written resolutions are so much more – binding, somehow!

Feb 11, 1957. More lovely news. My oration was judged best in the school and I get to give it next Monday at Pleasant Grove in the American Legion contest. Great fun!

Feb 13, 1957. If my handwriting is a bit more shaky than usual tonight, it's because my stomach is growling so hard my whole body shakes. It just so happens that I have not had anything to eat since noon. You see, tomorrow is Valentine's Day, and on the eve before, if you skip supper and pin five bay leaves on your pillow, you will dream of your future true lover. This should prove most interesting! Many of us are doing it. But good grief — I'm starving to death!

This delightful little bit of divination has been practiced by young women in one way or another for centuries. (See Keats' poem, "The Eve of St. Agnes.") But even customs much less ancient and honorable than this one should be recorded – they're great fun to look back on, for one thing, and they show certain aspects of the times in ways that big events and headlines never can.

Feb 16, 1957. I'm tired, tired, tired! I guess we did all right at Weber. At least I was among the top 20 or so out of 130. But there are more contests ahead of us.

"Weber" refers to the annual state speech competition held at Weber College in Ogden, Utah.

Feb 25, 1957. I wonder if I will live through this week. But that's the trouble: I know I will. No such comforting release as death.

Mar 7, 1957. I've been studying for the contest all day. I just hope I get an extemp in something I know about. Mr. Golightly is taking me up in the morning. It's at Cyprus High. Ah, how I wonder what I'll be writing in this diary twenty-four hours from now!

Mar 8, 1957. Well, the state semifinals were today, and I won first place. Now I go on to the finals in Salt Lake on the 19th. Forensic regional is the 18th. I hope I don't get them all mixed up!

Mr. G. is a very devoted and interesting husband. I want one just like him. Also, today he gave me the lead in his contest play. What's more, opposite me he may cast IT! All in all, today was very nice.

Notice that "He," fallen from grace, has become "It."

Mar 13, 1957. We voted today for Senior Personalities: Most Likely to Succeed, Be Remembered, Most Friendly, Amusing, Contributed Most, and Most Dreamed About. Anyway, for the paper [*April Fool issue*] we are having: Most Likely to Recede, Most Likely to be Dismembered, Most Fiendly, Most Abusing, and Most Screamed About. Summer is not far away. Neither is madness!

Mar 19, 1957. Of course the contest was today, and I — well, no, I didn't win. But after all, state finalist isn't so bad. A boy from Ogden won, and I think he should have, because he was really terrific. However, second place was given to the girl *I beat* at regionals. I don't see that at all!

Mar 20, 1957. We had play practice, and it was hilarious. It and I went through our love scenes many times. We both just deteriorate when he has to clasp me and gaze soulfully into my eyes while saying, "And I shall always love you."

Wheeeeeeeeeeeeeee, what fun!!

Mar 26, 1957. I placed first in region today! Tonight at play practice, Golightly explained to us what the "object" is in the play: a goal one builds up in one's mind that he seeks for and deems highly important, yet it is not. I've never seen such perfect parallelism in my life! It's so true. By the time the play is over, I shall be as immovable and recovered as anything.

Daddy will be operated on on Monday. We went to see him today.

Carol Lynn's mention of her father's operation raises an important point. While nobody wants to develop the whiney tone of a hypochondriac, recording every sniffle, ache, and ouch in a journal, it's a very smart move to include in your journal significant details of your medical history. Such details could be valuable or even life-saving someday. And on a lesser level, an entry reading "Had tetanus shot today at clinic" could save you the discomfort of another tetanus shot a year or two later because it would establish that you'd had one within the safe time period. Record allergic reactions, medication that you take on doctor's orders, major symptoms, major illnesses, operations, and so on.

Mar 30, 1957. I brought It's coat home today to fix for the play (the coat with *my* black still on it!) and have been wearing it all night.

Apr 9, 1957. I have just been confronted with the possibility of winning either a thousand dollars or a trip to Washington, D. C. It's another contest — all about Alexander Hamilton. It's so neat to even think about.

Apr 11, 1957. Today was very nice. We went to the Manti Temple to be baptized for the dead. It was beautiful. The entire day was *neat*! I received a letter from BYU saying I am receiving a scholarship.

Apr 13, 1957. We did it! We took state! WE RECEIVED THE SWEEPSTAKES AWARD! We received a beautiful trophy and plaques. Also, I received one of the four awards for best performance. . . . We hauled the trophy all over town, took pictures, and had a ball.

Apr 15, 1957. Mr. G. got very upset at me today, and it really makes me mad. It's really a matter of principle — whether or not everyone and their dog should be in the yearbook picture of the state drama champions. He shoved in a few bystanders who just barely got to regionals. I maintained the opinion of the group that it should be exclusive. As a result, he now has me branded as a "glory-hog," which really and truly makes me feel bad. However, I still cannot see his reasoning. Today was really a putrid day. Mainly, I have discovered that J. H. has now pushed his ugly face into this recent Hamilton contest. I'm ashamed to admit it, but I hate J. I hate hate hate hate hate hate hate hate hate hate him! I hate everything today, and most of all, myself for doing so.

A self-respecting journal records the bad days as well as the good.

May 11, 1957. Well, I have a date for the dance — M.! I've been alternating between rejoicing and mourning ever since. I'd die if I didn't get to go to the dance; but I also knew I'd die if I had to go with M. again. He is really better than nothing, I guess (I keep telling myself). Really, I'm going to make myself have a ball in spite of it all.

May 15, 1957. Oh, by the way, I won $1,000 today. Really and truly — a thousand-dollar scholarship to the college of my choice. Yes, I won the Alexander Hamilton Bicentennial Oratorical Contest — in fact, I won both prizes. The money and a trip to Philadelphia to participate in the national contest. Needless to say, I am quite thrilled. Also at the Awards Assembly, I won the "Best Actress" award, which thrilled me nearly as much. . . . All in all, today was just really great.

17

Tomorrow is graduation, and I won't even try to express my sentiments.

Oh, try, Carol Lynn, try! As we'll see, CLW soon becomes adept at expressing her sentiments, even though it's never exactly an easy thing to do. As for your diary – express, express!

Jun 14, 1957. Up at 4:30 and at the station at 5:50. I found my way to my seat and sat a while; seat 16, car 12, *California Zephyr.* Soon I went to breakfast — $1.50. . . . We're now in Spanish Fork Canyon, and I'm trying desperately to enjoy my trip; I think I will.

Your travel details may. seem commonplace, but record them: in a few decades, they will seem quaint and also faintly romantic.

Jun 19, 1957. We got up this morning and went to the Hamilton Exhibition. It was really interesting. We saw all his personal possessions, etc. Then we went sightseeing all over Washington and went to the Senate chambers. They didn't accomplish much. We all met Vice-President Nixon and had our pictures taken with him. In the afternoon we met President Eisenhower. I was right next to him and we had pictures taken. I'll be on the front page of the Philadelphia paper tomorrow. We then came directly to Philadelphia by bus. It's even hotter and more humid here, I think.

Maybe nothing is more of a challenge for a diarist than finding something meaningful to say about a brief encounter with a celebrity. "She looks younger than she does on television" is about the best most of us can come up with. The problem is that even United States presidents are not likely to make historic statements while posing for pictures or simply greeting contest winners – so what do you write, except that you shook hands or posed? One thing you can do is look for – and record – tiny details that may be, in themselves, unimportant, but that will help you fix that moment in your mind so that forever after, when you reread your journal entry, the whole scene will come back, intact. For example: "On his desk was a tiny, hand-carved sailboat. I wonder what its significance is to him?" or "She had a wonderful laugh – deep and throaty and unexpected in someone as small as she."

Jun 25, 1957. I wrote to Yellowstone and requested employment for the remainder of the season. Also I wrote to the girls there.

Jun 26, 1957. I ironed somewhat today. But most all day was spent compiling the many poems I've written during my life. I didn't know

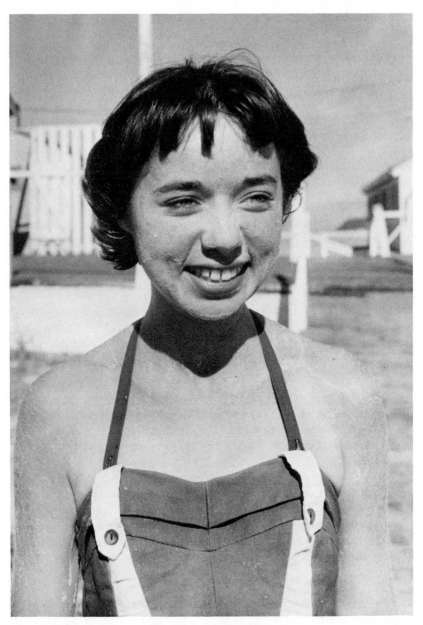

At the Great Salt Lake

there were so many. A few good ones, some fair ones, and many poor ones.

Carol Lynn obviously did something important that many of us neglect; she kept track of things! Here we see her "compiling" poems that she had written over the years – not only written, but preserved. In the years between the ages of twelve and, say, twenty-five, most people move around a good deal, what with travel, work, school, first apartments, and so forth. Don't let your diaries, important letters, photographs, artwork, or whatever get lost or thrown out during this time. Get a couple of good file boxes, sturdy footlockers, or other trustworthy containers, and keep your valuable papers safe. When you store them (with family or friends), make it clear that they are important, and should be treated that way.

Jul 4, 1957. Today, obviously, was the Fourth of July. Just five years ago I was burned by the fireworks falling on me. They've had fireworks shows every year since then, but nobody's ever been burned besides me. We leave tomorrow. I sometimes think diaries are useless. One hasn't words or time enough to write anything of worth.

Obviously, CLW decided in favor of diaries. Here's an interesting question on the subject: Did she stick with her journals because she was a good writer? or did she become a good writer partly because she persevered at writing in her journals? or both? In any case, she evidently made the time, and found the words as time went by.

Jul 22, 1957. I have now been at Yellowstone some two weeks and am probably enjoying it. The kids seemed glad to see me when I arrived, and I sure was glad to see them. I really don't mind the work, but I wish I had a station of my own. I'll get $75 per month and a bonus if I stay till the end.

We've been playing lovely tricks on each other — bleach in bubble bath, nail polish on soap and bobby pins, vinegar on toothbrush, shortsheeting beds, "Cheer" [*detergent*] in beds, potato chips in beds, newspapers in beds, pinning up beds, removing mattresses, sewing up clothes, ammonia on pillows, and many more, past and future. We do have fun together. I'll write every day from now on.

Aug 8, 1957. Made $1.25 in tips today.

Aug 18, 1957. Selene, Joan, and I went for a walk and saw the falls (upper and lower) and the canyon. It's just beautiful! I've never seen anything prettier, ever. I memorized "O Captain, My Captain." I have been for several days, and intend to keep on memorizing a poem a day.

Aug 19, 1957. Selene and I went horseback riding — for free. It all comes from buttering up the cowboys.

Aug 29, 1957. Last night I sat in the closet (where I am now) and read much of *Adam Bede*. I was so captivated and enthralled I couldn't lay it down. The stark tragedy just really cut me, and I suffered real torment. Tonight at work I finished the book. It is one of the best I have ever read.

Sep 3, 1957. We packed. The room looks so very funny and sad being all bare and clean. We really scrubbed it down. Joan and I went over to hear the band a few minutes. I weighed myself — with heavy clothes on, I am 119 — an all-time high! Goodbye, Yellowstone!

Sep 4, 1957. I might have been sad leaving, did not my life pass too quickly to be sentimental.

"If I had time, I would be sad"

During the last week of September 1957, the newspaper headlines throughout the United States reported that Arkansas Governor Orval Faubus had barred Negroes from entering Little Rock's Central High School, in defiance of three federal desegregation orders. The integration of the public schools would remain a major issue throughout the fifties and into the sixties. Utah, however, with an extremely small Negro population, was largely untouched by this controversy, and in Provo, Carol Lynn began her freshman year on a serene and untroubled campus. The biggest thing on her mind was which of two plays to try out for. Tryouts, rehearsals, and dramatic performances would consume countless hours during the next four years. Her diaries reveal that while she was a conscientious student who kept her grades high and who maintained her scholarship with ease, the smell of the greasepaint was overpowering. Drama took center stage in her life, and stayed there throughout her years as an undergraduate and graduate student.

Sep 26, 1957. Orientation was fine — so many freshmen: 3,500! It was neat — we all stood and sang (without books) "The Spirit of God Like a Fire Is Burning." Had tests and lots of speeches. Selene and I (after much inward strife) tried out for Gledhill's play *Anastasia.*

Sep 27, 1957. It's my birthday today! I'm hoping to get a clearer perspective during this, my eighteenth year.

Sep 28, 1957. Dr. Gledhill posted the final tryouts list: I was on it! I read again for him; I wish I'd get the charwoman part.

Sep 30, 1957. I received a part in *Anastasia* — the charwoman. It's quite small, but an excellent character role.

Oct 1, 1957. I registered today! Dr. Mitchell was my advisor. My first class is at 10 A.M. Book of Mormon, Dance, Speech, History, and English.

Oct 2, 1957. My first day of school is over. I think I'll make it!

Oct 6, 1957. In Sunday School they discussed what a wife had to do to make a happy home. It indeed painted a dark picture. I don't intend to go through life acting the part of a stupid, inefficient, fragile idiot to make men think they're superior — they're not! I doubt if I shall ever find the type of man I want — or one who'll want me — as an equal, not an inferior ego-builder.

Oct 7, 1957. I've been quite upset tonight. I'm so dissatisfied with myself and wrapped in self-pity. I do wish I knew what to do with my life.

"What will I do with my life?" This quest for direction becomes one of the chief themes in CLW's diaries. You may enjoy tracing its development and resolution.

Oct 9, 1957. Got first English theme back — B. Went to dance class and am quite stiff.

Oct 10, 1957. Wrote English theme today and late tonight. Not awfully good. Everybody's got the Asiatic flu!

Oct 13, 1957. Sunday School was quite good today. Still talking about family relationships — duty of wife.

Oct 17, 1957. Afternoon tried to write theme but slept an hour with face in sun — extremely enjoyable. Memorized a bit of *Thanatopsis*.

Oct 19, 1957. Put up the rest of the grape juice today. Play practice at one o'clock and then to Thea Alexis meeting. Practice again at seven o'clock, dress rehearsal — quite good. I stayed and watched the rest of the play. I've a lovely costume, quaint little hat and all. Just two more rehearsals.

Oct 23, 1957. Opening night, and it really went quite well. 'Bout full house. It's awfully fun to do.

23

Oct 25, 1957. A long, long day. (To bed at 4:30.) Cast party — good. Helped with Theta Alpha Phi's float. At 2:30, Tom (Macaulay) and I walked down to my house to get the car so I could take him home. We then decided to see Dr. Mitchell's play off for Pocatello. Threw pennies at Liane's window. It was all a real ball! He is undoubtedly the funniest boy (and the giddiest) I've ever met. HMMMMMMMMMMMMMMMMMMMMMMMMMMMMMMMM!

Oct 27, 1957. Oh, my! I could very easily go into a coma over Prince Paul (Tom). But it's too dangerous! I must try to keep control of myself.

Nov 1, 1957. Hurriedly typed over English theme. I wish I could once be completely satisfied with a theme.

Nov 2, 1957. It snowed for the first time today. Really beautiful. Each snowfall really undoes me emotionally.

One of the delayed-reaction pleasure of journals is comparing notes with another diarist – the "Where-were-you-on-this day?" sort of thing. Four years older than Carol Lynn, I was a first-year graduate student at BYU in 1957, having received my bachelor of arts degree at the sunny University of Arizona. This same November 2 was a big day for me, and for the same reason – the snow, my first snowfall in many, many years. I took countless snapshots and somehow never forgot the date. And right around the corner from my lodgings in Provo, a friend I wouldn't meet for several years yet was enjoying that same snow, and recording its impact on her.

Nov 7, 1957. Today I won two tickets to the Academy Theater by knowing who wrote "O Captain, My Captain!" Walt Whitman, of course. [*CLW won the tickets by calling in the correct answer to a radio station that was running an on-the-air quiz.*]

Nov 9, 1957. Play practice at nine o'clock. Washed windows all morning and worked all afternoon. My hands smell Purex-y, and I'm tired.

Nov 10, 1957. I was just reading last year's November 10 entry. It was a sad day, and most memorable. Happily, I can now wonder why I was so upset. Since I'm now all cured of it, I feel no old nostalgia. Had a very good missionary lesson in church today.

Scientists can look at a cross-section of a tree, and by counting the circular rings can mark the growth and determine the age of the tree. They

24

can even read the tree's history, up to a point, by spotting evidence of a fire or an insect plague in the shape and size of the growth rings. Journals can work the same way, showing the writer his or her own growth and witnessing to healing that has taken place. There's a special excitement in this process, because for most of us, the best lessons are the ones we teach ourselves, and that's exactly what happens as we write and then reread our journals.

Nov 15, 1957. Today was quite my day: I ran into yon Cassius (Tom) twice and talked to him both times.

Nov 19, 1957. Woke Dick up in the Reserve Library again. Missed seeing Tom completely. Went to the Heber J. Grant Oratorical Contest this morning — very good, although I didn't agree with the judges.

Nov 22, 1957. Got my English theme back — A! He read it in class and also wants a copy for his files. I'm very happy about it.

Nov 28, 1957. Thanksgiving. Slept in, fixed a big ham dinner, and ate, ate, ate. Warren put clothes starch instead of cornstarch in the pie, but it was good anyway.

Nov 29, 1957. Pajamas weren't dry, so I studied history until 1 A.M., and they were dry.

Oh, the trials of pre-drier days! Actually, of course, home washers and driers had been invented by this time, and most families had a washing machine of one sort or another, but driers were not routine appliances in the average home until a few years later.

Dec 6, 1957. Yesterday Dr. Hansen had his secretary call up and ask me to try out for his play. I did — last night, this afternoon, and all night tonight. I don't know yet who I am — but we're rehearsing all day tomorrow. *Blithe Spirit* — really hilarious.

Dec 7, 1957. Nothing but play rehearsals all day. We blocked and went over and over Act One — about got it memorized. I have the part of Ruth.

Dec 16, 1957. My English teacher called me in for consultation on my polygamy theme. [*The subject assigned was "A Fate Worse Than Death."*] He gave me an A on it, but wanted to straighten me out. We had an enjoyable discussion — but that's all. [*CLW did not change her opinion!*]

25

Dec 17, 1957. There have been five days this quarter that I haven't been tied up in a play.

Dec 23, 1957. Did my Christmas shopping today — also made ten candles. What a mess! They're quite pretty, though.

Dec 24, 1957. Christmas Eve! I really can't believe it. Rehearsal this morning. Cleaned house, wrapped and delivered presents. Watched TV, filled Daddy's and Warren's stockings. Wish I still believed in Santa Claus.

Dec 26, 1957. Play rehearsal all day. And we went on tonight. Apparently it went over quite well. It was all quite jolly, and I even got to wear Mama's wedding rings. I am quite tired.

Dec 27, 1957. Read a beautiful poem — from *The City of Dreadful Night,* by James Thompson.

Dec 28, 1957. I woke up at death's door this morning. Had a miserable cold. Went to Health Center and got a penicillin shot and some pills. Slept the rest of the day — ate lemons, inhaled, took pills, sprayed Anahist, rubbed Vicks, and took aspirin. Fortunately my voice was not affected much. Play went very well. In fact, we're playing over all next week "due to popular demand."

Dec 29, 1957. I do wish just one of my castles in the air would one day materialize!

Dec 30, 1957. Gyp [*the family dog*] didn't get any better, so Daddy called the pound and they came and got him. I guess he is now passed over to his reward. I'm very sad — we've had him about ten years. When I have time, I shall grieve about it.

The play went quite poorly tonight — bad audience, Charles goofed his lines, technicians were off. And to top everything, we ran out of gray spray, and I had to do my hair with shoe polish!

Dec 31, 1957. New Year's Eve. Slept in, cleaned house, ironed, etc. Play went quite well — my voice was full of pneumonia, but okay. . . . If I had time, I would be sad.

Jan 11, 1958. Today is the birthday of Alexander Hamilton! Fine old fellow that he was. If Aaron Burr hadn't shot him, he'd be 201 years old. One moment of reverent silence. . . .

With Selene Sandberg (now Selene Oates)

Remember that the Hamilton scholarship CLW won is, in part, financing her education.

Jan 18, 1958. Ushered at the play and then came home. I couldn't stand to see him [*Tom*] up there on stage making love to those women. Had a lonely walk home. Stood on the top of the hill (where we were before) and sang "When You Wish Upon a Star." The snow was beautiful, and all very dramatic. The victory bell is just this minute ringing. I guess we won our game. Oh, I wish I'd win mine!

Feb 4, 1958. Been reading my poetry book and have memorized "Spring and Fall" by Hopkins. I like it!

Feb 5, 1958. Vibrated in dance and had soup with Marilyn. Also handed in two poems to the *Wye* [*campus literary magazine*]. I felt so dumb, I wanted to tear them up and run. Oh, well, I've seen worse things published.

Feb 19, 1958. All the social units are initiating their "goats." I wish I could join one — it looks so jolly. But if one is a speech major, one can't have time for much else.

27

Feb 21, 1958. Strange things are happening. Yesterday Tom called me about José Greco. I think all he wanted was my car, but anyway —.

Feb 23, 1958. Went to Selene's and had her cut my hair. Sat afterwards and talked about what to do this summer. I guess I'll stay here, try to find a job, do *Blithe Spirit* again, try to help with *Sand in Their Shoes*, and, I hope, go back with the Hill Cumorah Pageant. Maybe one session of summer school, too.

Mar 10, 1958. It's only two o'clock and I'm beastly tired. Rehearsal at six. Tom came late, and I helped him make up. Snuck into the Press and got a *Wye* magazine. Carleen got her poem in it. Someday I'm going to write a good poem, too.

Mar 18, 1958. Tonight I pulled many more white hairs out of my head.

Mar 19, 1958. Dropped in on Dr. Clark to get research paper and themes. I got an A out of the class. He keeps telling me he wants me to major in English. Read entire three parts of *Mourning Becomes Electra* by Eugene O'Neill — really good. Extremely morbid, but quite intriguing.

Mar 20, 1958. Read four plays today, all O'Neill's: *Ah, Wilderness, Welded, Gold,* and *The First Man.*

Throughout her college years, Carol Lynn read many plays each week, as well as poems, novels, history, and much Church material. We haven't room to give more than a sampling of the titles. Be sure to record your own reading, and your reaction to what you read.

Mar 26, 1958. Went to Selene's for a little haircut and motherly lecture on "All work and no play makes Selene and Carol Lynn dull girls."

Mar 28, 1958. I composed a lovely poem today — shall here record it:

Comes the First Breath of Spring

Lady Spring exhales,
     with fragrant breath,
Blowing perfume, music, and roses.

> But as my luck goes,
>> Even Spring's first breath
> Is naught but halitosis!

I like it.

Mar 31, 1958. Tried out for *Thunder Rock* today. . . . I do wish I could get the part of Miss Kirby — a man-hating suffragette. Tonight, a rare experience. Thea Alexis group went to the State Mental Hospital to visit a ward. We were oriented first, and then went into the Day Room where all the patients were sitting around. Soon the whole ward was quite improved. Nearly every one of the patients loosened up and played games — checkers, horseshoes, tossing a ball, etc. Or dancing and talking with the girls. I think this kind of contact really helps them — and does wonders for the outsiders, too.

Apr 1, 1958. Only flunked a psych test today — first C I've ever gotten. Studied psych all afternoon. Made pizza pie for supper. Was called back for final tryouts tonight. Read again for Miss Kirby — I really like the part. He'll post the cast tomorrow.

Apr 2, 1958. Well, I got into the play. He didn't list who we were to play, but I'm sure I'm Miss Kirby. I think she is the most challenging of the three female parts. I'm quite happy about it. Ever since Friday, I've had some sort of panicky feeling — as if I had to write two more paragraphs of a theme and the bell was just about to ring! Undoes me!

Apr 13, 1958. Aunt Mamie and Uncle Wesley came down and brought me the book they had for my high school graduation present. Marjorie Wilson's *Complete Book of Charm.* I shall now commence to read it. I do believe I need it more than botany.

Apr 16, 1958. Got my letter of acceptance from H.I.H. [*Harold I. Hansen, BYU professor of dramatic arts and director of the annual Hill Cumorah Pageant*] about Hill Cumorah Pageant. It should be really neat.

Apr 17, 1958. Had costume fitted — it's only beautiful — gray wool huge skirt (with top), long sleeves and crimson puff sleeve. Also got umbrella.

Apr 21, 1958. Stake conference. Elder Moyle presided. Big discussion on too much "going steady." Well, that's one problem I don't have to worry about!

By this point, CLW is at least recording the subject matter of conferences and devotionals.

May 6, 1958. Slept all afternoon and then the final dress rehearsal. My hair fell off completely in the middle of a big tense scene! Hope tomorrow goes well!

May 7, 1958. Play opened, and I felt really strange. I don't feel that I did very well at all. I wish I knew what to do.

May 9, 1958. I've kinda hit a new low. Tonight at meeting before performance, Dr. Hansen told me it's still my fault I get such an audience reaction on Miss Kirby's going to find a husband in Deseret. He said if I create sufficient mood and depth, I wouldn't get more than the slightest murmur. I tried to keep it more inward and intense, but got the same reaction — just about broke down. All the cast seems to sympathize and say it's not my fault, but Hansen says it is. I can't even make a joke to relieve the pressure, and that means it is really bad.

May 10, 1958. Well, the play's over, and I feel quite good about it. I don't know quite how, but I didn't even get a murmur from the audience during my Deseret bit. It made me feel quite good.

May 11, 1958. Church and all. Mother's Day program. Took some lilacs out to the cemetery. [*To her mother's grave.*]

May 18, 1958. Have been thinking, wondering, wondering, wishing all day. Maybe this whole thing is all in my head instead of my heart. I half hope so — but then I don't know of a more stimulating way to suffer! All I can say is that if a broken heart and a contrite spirit can get me to heaven — I'm halfway there!

If you're a little vague as to just what "this whole thing" refers to, you're not alone! Faithful as she is in giving full details about most topics she treats in her journals, at this stage CLW is deliberately cloudy and cryptic about the specifics of her romantic attachments. One reason may have been her feeling that if she spelled out particulars of an attachment that seemed to be developing, she might "jinx" the desired outcome.

Jun 2, 1958. Mrs. Glover gave a very inspiring little speech in dance about the creative act being the closest thing to godliness.

Jun 5, 1958. Said goodbye to Tom twice today. At Speech Center and over hill after film. Nothing tender even, just goodbye.

Life Mask party. Berta made me a mask — nobody else dared have one made. I lay down in the hall, with paper all over and vaseline on my face, and cardboard all around, straws in my nose. She piled gunk all over my face, and I stayed there for a long time (fifteen minutes). Then they took it off — pulled all my lovely eyelashes out with it. It sure is an ugly thing. Must see how masks turn out. My eyeballs sting and I'm tired and emotionally distraught.

Jul 25, 1958. [*En route to Cumorah Pageant*]. We have just left Rock Springs [*Wyoming*], where we stopped for lunch. Some of us went down to a grocery and stockpiled goodies to save money. We are on three buses, 114 people in all. We've been asked to always call each other Elder and Sister. We each introduced ourselves on the P. A. system and sang for several hours — I'm just hoarse. We stopped at Evanston, and I got a map on which I'm tracing our route.

Jul 29, 1958. Am now sitting in O'Donnell's Hotel Restaurant waiting for a bit of food I hardly expect to get. All of us converged upon the little place, which obviously is used to serving only a few stray customers. We finally were served our food: a little bowl of Post Toasties. That was after I had devoured a rose, chrysanthemum, and napkin. Actually, we had been there over two hours before our food arrived.

I'm now lying in my very bed at my very residence. We sang "Come, Come Ye Saints," approaching the hill, and just as we were singing the fourth verse, the Angel Moroni came into sight. We went directly to the Palmyra Chapel and stood in line to register.

Our family is very nice — all ten of them. It's an old big house with one bathroom among all of us. I'm in a room with one girl, four in the next room, and two in the hall.

Jul 31, 1958. The three-cent stamp is no more. Has gone up to four cents. Study classes all morning and afternoon in the woods. I gave a lesson — the apostasy. Converted a tree.

Today Lynn and I wrote each other letters so we wouldn't be left out of tomorrow's mail call. I wrote her a letter from Elder Thurgood. It was quite a goody.

Aug 4, 1958. All morning long I was in beard-making. I made Elder White's beard (Abinadi) and helped on several others. Got rather frustrated and all, but it was fun. Afternoon, I coated them again with

31

latex. We also went up to the top of the Hill and visited Moroni. Also, we went up to Stage Four and saw Chuck and his Lamanite dancers practice. Then we slept on the lawn down by the trailer with the blare of trumpets in our ears — they're continually practicing.

Aug 7, 1958. Had testimony meeting all day in the Grove. In the afternoon, Hugh B. Brown was there, also Albert Tuttle; both spoke to us. Dr. and Mrs. Hansen also spoke. We then came home for a little while, ate bread and milk, grabbed costumes, and left for the Hill. Lynn and I tended the information booth, giving out pamphlets, selling Books of Mormon and postcards. We then gathered on either side of the Hill to get ready for the Pageant. Got dressed. Dr. Hansen came over and we had prayer. Governor Harriman was there and gave a welcome address, as did Brother Brown. Brother Tuttle offered prayer, and we began.

The trumpeters got through perfectly. It was sprinkling very slightly, and ceased and increased alternately. When our Lamanite scene came, the rain continually increased and the wind blew until I thought we would all crumple up and die. I'll not soon forget the stark drama of that night. Just as Lamoni's dance got underway, the lights went out. We continued on for a while in darkness, rain, wind, and makeshift lighting. Suddenly we heard the voice of Dr. Hansen interrupting with "regrets that we must close the Pageant and invite you back for a lovely show tomorrow night." We were all very heartbroken and didn't know why the Lord hadn't let the Pageant progress without difficulty. Quite an unhappy night.

Aug 9, 1958. The Pageant went very well. Started off at about 6:30 A.M. for home.

Aug 14, 1958. Arrived home about nine o'clock. Trip was just really wonderful. Stayed up a while and talked to Martha. So good to sleep in a bed and pajamas again. Found letter from Tom waiting for me — he's planning to come back to school this fall.

Aug 23, 1958. Gave "The Waltz" for Oak Hills Seventies party. Forgot next-to-last paragraph. Ate chicken dinner there. Got my pictures of Pageant. Quite good.

"The Waltz" is a comic story by Dorothy Parker that CLW performed frequently as a reading. As time passed, Carol Lynn's dramatic skills became more in demand for church groups, women's clubs, literary leagues, and so

on. She read poetry, both her own and others', and did excerpts (or "cuttings") from many different plays.

Sep 1, 1958. Good grief, another month gone! Somewhat cleaned out closet and worked on clothes. Sunbathed three hours and read more of Dorothy Parker's short stories. Some I like, others not. I just love her poetry:

Two-volume Novel

The sun's gone dim,
And the moon's turned black,
For I loved him, and
He didn't love back.

Dorothy Parker left her mark on Carol Lynn, as she did on many another young writer. Parker's verse is generally short, ironic, witty, and clever, as is Carol Lynn's at its best.

It's fun to learn who the important influences were on those who achieve. In your own journals, be sure to note those whose examples you want to follow – whether it's in sports, music, art, writing, fashion, community service, or whatever.

"The drama of pain"

Early in September of 1958, the big news in America was the successful crossing beneath the polar ice cap by the nuclear submarine Nautilus. *In a lighter vein, popular magazines devoted pages to displaying the talents of the Miss America contestants, whose only nautical requirement was the wearing of bathing suits. Carol Lynn, like many Americans, followed this annual pageant eagerly each year, excited by the pomp and circumstance, deflated by what she saw as the glaring differences between herself and the beauty queens.*

Sep 6, 1958. Read last night until two o'clock — finished *The Mill on the Floss.* I just wept. Slept until nine o'clock. Cleaned house and all. Cleaned entire basement stairway. Tried to write a poem, didn't quite make it. Watched the Miss America Pageant — quite neat. Miss Mississippi won. I quite agreed. Miss Utah was among the ten semifinalists. It was all quite exciting. Wish I were beautiful.

Sep 22, 1958. I don't quite know how to say what I now have to say. Maybe if I were a more normal person, I wouldn't have any of these terrible frustrations. Maybe something's wrong with my whole mental makeup. I can't be realistic. But in the very same breath I'll always swear I don't *want* to be, nor could I if I did. After an upset like this when one part of my life is shattered, it so upsets the other parts that I think I'm completely on the wrong track. I want to change everything — me, my major — all. . . . A most frustrating part of all this is to know that soon I'll have forgotten it all and be close to where I was before.

34

Still, things are decidedly changed. I would certainly have a terrible life if I didn't half enjoy the drama of pain.

Sep 25, 1958. The first play of the season is *The Importance of Being Earnest* by Oscar Wilde. I checked it out tonight and read it. I quite like it. Some great female parts. I had almost decided to go into debate and not do plays for a while. But I'd so much rather act than debate.

Sep 27, 1958. I'm now in bed awaiting the ringing of the chimes announcing my very birth-hour. I was born at midnight. Marie is the only one who really remembered — made me a cake. M. A. remembered later and called. Also Daddy-o. Last day of orientation work. Tryouts for *Earnest*. I want very much to play Cecily, but I rather think that if I get anything, it'll be Lady Bracknell. The chimes are ringing — Happy Birthday! I wish I could say something profound — or even clear my thoughts. Just a note to my dear self of September 27, 1959, when I'll be twenty.
Dear Twenty:

I almost envy you, but am quite frightened for you — fully a whole year cannot go by without your becoming more you. But whether that is up or down may be yet undetermined. I wonder what you will have done in the department? You'll be a junior, now. I wonder if you will have found someone interesting or have developed a new platonic crush on someone new. I wonder what new friends you will have made, or maybe lost. Also, where the family will all be. Maybe lots of the group will be married and lots on missions. I guess Martha will have married Duane by now. There are a million things I wish would happen between now and then, but most of all, I hope I know you better than I do now.
Yours, as you are mine,
Sweet Nineteen.

Actually Carol Lynn later discovered she was born at 1 A.M., not midnight. Herein lies an interesting caution for diarists, and readers of diaries: Statistical information often gets mixed up as it is passed along, told and retold. For instance, I had an aunt who, against doctor's orders, had a baby; according to family tradition, she died shortly thereafter because of complications of childbirth. When I checked out official birth and death records, I found that the aunt had actually died ten years after her child was born! The rule is that you can trust first-hand reports more than second-hand ones, and on-the-spot reports better than later ones. In other words, CLW's mother would be a more reliable source than CLW herself, and her mother's diary at the time of the birth would be more reliable than a personal history account or a letter written by her ten or fifteen years later.

With this entry, CLW begins the annual custom of writing a letter to the self of a year hence. At this point, the letter is essentially one of wondering and hoping. But before long, her birthday becomes a time for challenge and commitment, with written goals set up for the year ahead. If this is an idea that appeals to you, why not try it in your journal? Incidentally, the chimes she mentions are those situated on the BYU campus; they sounded out the hours and could be heard clearly in many parts of Provo.

Sep 30, 1958. I'm in the play — Lady Bracknell.

Oct 15, 1958. We opened tonight — went quite well, I think.

Oct 16, 1958. Critique in the *Universe* [*BYU school newspaper*], pretty good. But it said I almost yelled, and "failed to play up nuances." Oh, well.

Oct 20, 1958. Forum assembly today: Senatorial candidates debated — Lee, Moss, and Watkins. Rather poor speeches... they hardly knew what they were talking about.

Oct 21, 1958. Talked to Dr. Woodbury about *Peter Pan*. He talks like he wants a boy or a little girl to play Peter. I told him to *forget it!*

Oct 30, 1958. We're going on tour for sure — December 5-12 — New Mexico and Arizona. Should be a real ball.

The play they were taking on tour was The Importance of Being Earnest.

Nov 20, 1958. Tom and I went to Salt Lake to see John Gielgud do his *Ages of Man* — cuttings from Shakespeare. Just a really terrific actor. Met him afterwards at reception (got his napkin and a crumb). I think he'll go places.

The last line is, of course, in jest. When CLW saw Gielgud in 1957, he had already "gone" everyplace an actor could go – he had only one rival for the title of greatest actor in the English-speaking world, and that was Laurence Olivier.

Nov 22, 1958. Read *The Lark* by Anouilh, and most of Schiller's *Maid of Orleans*.

Nov 27, 1958. Thanksgiving. Martha and I got up at five o'clock and put Thomasina (Turkey) on to cook. Baked pies and such. Reread *The Lark* and took notes on *Saint Joan*. When I get to heaven I'm going to look up old Joan.

Dec 25, 1958. Christmas Day. Glad New Year's is coming so I can repent methodically.

Dec 26, 1958. All evening long, I've been Peter Pan. No one was home — so I dressed up, made up, and made a stage out of the front room. Read and walked through the whole play reading Peter's lines aloud — had so much fun! Then I took his almost-final scene, memorized it, and rehearsed over and over. I love that play, and have never wanted anything so passionately as to play Peter. Even against such overwhelming odds, I'm going to fight to the finish!

Dec 31, 1958. It's now 1959 by nearly three hours, and gag a rag bag! Went to stake dance with an old missionary companion of Donald's. Really had a good time. He's an excellent dancer. I started to teach him the jitterbug.

"Gag a rag bag" was a popular slang expression that year. Its meaning was pretty general, often translating (roughly) into something like "My goodness!" One might say of a difficult situation or person, "It was enough to gag a rag bag." Bits of slang enliven a journal and make us smile as we look back at them later; it's surprising to see how quickly they become outdated.

Jan 15, 1959. Today . . . a most interesting discussion in English about "great men." Dr. Clark, after I pinned him down, told us that he would rather give us goals for living — the seeking after greatness, unrest, and dissatisfaction — as opposed to contentedness and normal happiness. Must think about it more!

Jan 18, 1959. I can't imagine a healthy nineteen-year-old making so much out of so little!

Jan 20, 1959. I waste time now that I haven't so much to do. Must get in play and keep occupied.

Jan 21, 1959. Banana [*Martha*] is using my pen to write to her mother, so I must use this pencil, which Time shall fade. Pity that my grandchildren reading this with bated breath shall miss even a day of my eventful life due to pencil smudges.

Have you ever groped your way through a letter or journal of yesteryear, wishing mightily that your ancestor had been a little more considerate of your eyes? Or, more seriously, have you ever lost a name or an important fact because an entry was illegible? Some journal-keepers today are even typing their entries – and surely their posterity will call them blessed for that – but you needn't go so far. Do use good paper, though, and ink rather than pencil. Speaking of ink, it may be fun to write in pink, purple, or green, but it's much less fun to read such colorful penmanship. Stick with blue or black.

Jan 27, 1959. *Matchmaker* tryouts were posted. Wish I knew for a surety that I'm not being foolish to skip them for the faint but magnetic hope of *Peter Pan*. In Mutual, discussed the human mind.

"Discussed the human mind" – and came to what conclusions? Popular opinions about philosophy, psychology, and other disciplines change rapidly; it's fun to keep track of the changes, so record a few of the details of discussions.

Jan 28, 1959. Great emotional and spiritual purge day — needn't recount details, because I'm not likely to forget it. I intend to hold my banner to the end . . . and "with God be the rest."

You guessed it: she forgot it!

Jan 31, 1959. A great day — the culmination of all these months of turmoil. Result: I'm going to play *The Matchmaker*. A great gain, but not offset by a great loss. *Peter Pan* will not be done this year. Dr. Gledhill called me in to see why I hadn't tried out [for The Matchmaker]. I explained it all and he said for me to come up and read for him this afternoon, at which time he would decide for sure, and then I could decide, too. He called back a little while later and said he wanted to use me. So he called Dr. Woodbury to see if he would like to consider me seriously for *Peter Pan*. Woodbury told him just what he had told me. Immediately after Gledhill called me back, however, Woodbury called and told me . . . that *Peter Pan* will not be presented this year . . . probably next year. So there is always a chance. *The Matchmaker* part is really cute, and will be most fun. I feel very flattered that he [*Gledhill*] should come to me like that. I'm afraid that many people will feel bad against me, because I've told them I intended to wait for *Peter*. Anyway, I'm most happy about it.

Feb 1, 1959. Fast day. Testimony meeting. For the first time in regular fast meeting, I bore my testimony. I'm very glad I did.

Feb 7, 1959. Tired! Play rehearsal all morning — slow. Went to Salt Lake to see *Elizabeth the Queen* with Mildred Dunnock. Really well done. Banana [*Martha*], Duane, Ron, Judy, Tom, and me. During intermission, Tom and I snuck from balcony to third row — neat! Went to the play this evening with Eldon. Really enjoyed it. Banana did especially well; best I've ever seen her.

I think it's silly to go out with boys just for the sake of going with them!

Feb 8, 1959. Just when I think I'm winning in the battle of the self, I suffer a relapse and grovel in waves of me!

Feb 14, 1959. Long day. Rehearsal all morning. Pretty good — we're all memorized. . . . Lots of housework, etc. Bought a plastic cover for the kitchen table — turquoise, really pretty. Did homework. Read Christina Rossetti's poetry. Tired, but comfortable tiredness after a long day of hard work and nine hours of good sleep approaching. (Monday I am going to the French film *Topaz* with "Vandergelder." No comment: whenever I do comment, things curdle.)

Feb 16, 1959. Went to French film with Fred ("Vandergelder"). Film was really out of it. Now I know why France is so deteriorated. Rather enjoyable, however.

Feb 18, 1959. Carl Sandburg spoke in assembly today — very enjoyable. . . .

Mar 11, 1959. Opening night. I think it went pretty well. Audience was okay. Warmed up gradually. Things such as Tom dropping Julia happened, but nothing serious.

Mar 24, 1959. Took Fred home and talked an hour with him. (I hope the dreams I've created today do not find themselves on the same shelf as the other fairy tales I've written.)

Mar 27, 1959. P. A. Christensen read his cutting of *Romeo and Juliet* in class. Watched *four* erosion movies in geology. Tibet, Larry Roupe.

Apr 3, 1959. Martha and Duane left early and went to Salt Lake to be married. I haven't even seen them yet. Finished poem and left it for them: "Ode on Banana's Finally Leaving the Bunch," or "Gee, I'm Glad We Married Duane!" Quite lovely in three cantos. . . . Banana is gone — funny!

Apr 13, 1959. After geology, Larry [*Roupe*] came home with me, and we ate soup and read a play.

Apr 15, 1959. Larry missed geology, and I him.

Apr 18, 1959. Mary Anne and I went downtown to buy birthday presents for Selene and Joan. Sweetbriar's was having a sale, and I bought two dresses — a darling royal-blue suit-dress and a red jersey sheath. $3.50 and $4!

Swift as most of life's changes are, few are as fleet as changing prices! Another reason detailed old diaries make such poignant reading. From time to time, as you write your own record, make note of some typical prices on food, clothing, amusements, and so on.

Apr 19, 1959. My imagination has been going a mile a minute all day. I'm quite afraid to contemplate!

Apr 20, 1959. A most strange Larry day. I don't know how to explain it, so I won't try. A great amount of way far ups and one huge down. I feel like my whole soul is rolled up in a hard ball pounding away at my stomach.

From this point on, throughout college and graduate school, three young men recur in CLW's diaries: Fred, Larry, and Tom. They do not follow one after another in time, but rather all three weave in and out from time to time, with one becoming the central figure toward the end.

Apr 21, 1959. Spent all afternoon with Larry. We rode down to the park on his bicycle and studied in the sun. Then ate lunch at the bakery and went in the Old Cottage Bookstore. He bought me a little *Sonnets from the Portuguese* and wrote in it. I feel like I have fuzzy glasses on that dim my brain.

May 11, 1959. Rather a significant day. I should be tremendously wrought up and disturbed, but I'm really not. Great misunderstanding with Larry. He was late, so I left. . . . Either I'm still numb, or a comforting spirit is hovering nigh.

May 12, 1959. A most strange day of which I am rather proud. For the first time I have countered with positive action the tendency to slip into waves of despondency and grovel in self-pity. I very frankly spelled out the score as I saw it, and I'm sure I completely flabbergasted Larry. I'm sure I'll feel rather silly about it, but I had to do something. After the little episode, we came to my house, ate lunch on the patio, rode home, and parted on rather good terms. (I'm acting so mature about this whole darn thing that I can hardly believe it!)

May 23, 1959. Got patches with Larry for his jacket. Rode around and went down to rodeo for a while. Had big argument and parted most unfriendly. Sick!

Jun 2, 1959. I just sit here and ferment in my own virtue.

Jun 4, 1959. School is all over! Larry was supposed to call me tonight from Laramie — hasn't yet.

June 25, 1959. Wrote another poem tonight, also untitled:

> Is this the reward spring romance brings?
> This omnibus of sundry things
> That bathe in pain the mortal soul,
> And shroud the poor, defenseless whole
> Of being in a stifling cape
> From which is offered no escape?
> Why, then, I draw but one conclusion;
> A germ of wisdom from illusion:
> Though prize is got
> And race is run,
> 'Tis better to have loved and lost
> Than to have loved and won.

Jun 26, 1959. I just truly don't know what to think about Larry. What do I do now? He came into the costume shop for his fitting — black and green and beautiful. Couldn't thread a needle for ten minutes afterwards.

Jul 9, 1959. "So I smile and say, 'When a lovely flame dies, smoke gets in your eyes.' " [*Lyrics of a song popular in 1959.*] Things with Larry are so bad that I'm physically sick.

Jul 17, 1959. Larry saw us out at the lake. I don't think he knew we were following him.

Jul 22, 1959. Went over Larry's lines with him. Cooked lunch, corn on the cob and hamburgers. Drove him home. Sent sixteen postcards of well wishes to him from everyone from Angel Moroni to Fidel Castro.

41

Jul 29, 1959. Found Tom Macaulay's Theta pin in Lost and Found. Wore it all day and told Larry I was pinned to Tom. I don't think he believed me, but it was interesting.

Aug 4, 1959. Was feeling bad all day about Larry. Then about 3:30 a package was delivered to me. Flowers from Larry! Seven red roses in a corsage: "Good luck. Love, Jazbo." I was most overwhelmed and could hardly contain myself. Show opened. [*The Heiress*]. Went quite well, I thought.

Aug 9, 1959. Selene and I drove up the canyon. Sat on little island and read Walt Whitman. Larry called — glad I wasn't home. He thinks we're going steady — but only on Sundays.

A great many young people, inspired by Carol Lynn and other Church poets, are interested in doing some creative writing of their own – which is terrific! The Church needs all the good writers it can find. But some beginners make the mistake of thinking they can write good poetry without ever having read any. Notice how often Carol Lynn spends time with the works of great poets – and remember that these excerpts give only a sampling of all she read.

Aug 10, 1959. Banana, Duane, Larry, and I went up the canyon and ate corn, roasted marshmallows, swung in swings, walked, etc. Tremendous fun — one of the best times we've ever had.

The details of how people spend their leisure, what they do on holidays and vacations, change with time and circumstance. In the 1970s, junior high and high school students often passed spare hours roaming up and down the promenades of large shopping malls; details like that, even twenty years later, may appear a quaint and interesting pastime. Try to include in your journal details of a typical family get-together, a typical evening out with a member of the opposite sex, a typical vacation trip by car, and so forth.

Aug 11, 1959. Sunbathed after class. Finished *The Iceman Cometh* — quite powerful. Made pies. Letter from Tom. Also read *Look Homeward, Angel, Medea* (Robinson Jeffers), and *Ethan Frome*, by Edith Wharton. Really liked it.

Aug 15, 1959. Spent all evening writing to Larry a letter that I will never send. All the other times like this, I've only been upset to the point of emotional vibrancy. Tonight I am physically sick.

Aug 16, 1959. I could not live through this weekend again — I would

As Catherine in The Heiress

have both a physical and a mental breakdown. I must really write a story about this — it's unbelievable. He had spent the weekend in Rawlins, Wyoming, with his father, who is dying of throat cancer. He had received a letter from his stepmother and left without calling me. The whole thing is so comically tragic as to sound fabricated, but it's a fact. He came over and I fixed supper for him — looked at my Alexander Hamilton things, and walked around school. Beautiful, just beautiful!

Aug 19, 1959. Too frustrated to write. Canned tomatoes all day. L. was supposed to come over — didn't. His mother arrived in town. (I didn't know it then.) Again I went off the deep end and mingled my tears with the rain.

Aug 24, 1959. I so hate to write this page that I'm doing it on the 25th. Larry is gone. He went to L. A. for a while and will go to New York. There are so many things I wanted to say to him, but I couldn't.

Sep 5, 1959. Spent entire day with Hardings in Salt Lake — Sunset Beach. Haven't been in the lake since I was a child, and I really enjoyed it. Just rolled into a position of prenatal security, closed my eyes, bobbed on the water wrapped in complete oblivion, and dissolved into nonentity.

Sep 6, 1959. Read many things — Wilder's short plays; *The Innocents. The Cocktail Party* by T. S. Eliot. Enjoyed them all with four pieces of honey-soaked bread.

> Words to Be Inscribed on the Warm Side of a Locket
>> I wish that I could weep for us.
>> A two-fold misery
>> Lends dignity to tears that fall.
>> But no — I weep for only me.

What's the most interesting thing about this entry? For many readers, it would be those four pieces of honey-soaked bread. Such homey little details make the difference between a black-and-white effect or Technicolor. Carol Lynn's complete diaries are filled with such details — accounts of encounters with spiders (she loathed them!) or moments of pure pleasure when she could get her hands on an avocado (she adored them!).

A colleague of mine told how as a young missionary he would put only the "important" details in his journals, but fortunately would often include the vivid little "unimportant" details in his letters to family and friends. "The letters now make by far the more interesting reading," he says.

Sep 7, 1959. Worked all day to celebrate Labor Day. Spent all evening reading letters that Mama sent to Daddy while they were engaged. Much of the writing sounds like what I might say — amazing! Unbelievable to think of them being young and in love. Wonder what kind of love letters I would write if ever given the occasion.

Most of us grow up with the real, if unexamined, feeling that the world really began the day we were born. When we discover, as CLW did in this instance, that people a generation or a century before us also loved, hated, were jealous, frustrated, silly, or scared, the human bond, as well as the family bond, tightens a little. Journals and diaries link the generations via a paper-and-ink chain that can be stronger than time or distance.

Sep 9, 1959. H. I. [*Hansen*] cast the play [*The Man Who Came to Dinner*] today. I didn't get any of the really fun parts. I play Mrs. Stanley, the lady of the house. We go on in *one week*! Looked through my old diaries and things.

Sep 14, 1959. I've never seen a play so completely unready three days before the performance. We just now blocked the third act. Our lead man almost has the first act memorized.

Sep 15, 1959. Rehearsed morning and night. Cleaned kitchen and fridge in the afternoon. Kruschev arrived in Washington today.

We do not go to diaries and journals to learn about the broad events of world and national history (unless the diarist is involved in making that history); these records are rightly personal ones. But jottings from time to time about what's going on in the world give a truer picture of the context of the life, and add dimension to that life and to the events of history.

Sep 17, 1959. One thing I hope: That I don't and won't underestimate myself and my capacities.

Sep 18, 1959. Opening night — really a nightmare!

Sep 19, 1959. Play went rather well — much better than last night. I suddenly realized that I should be wearing wedding rings, so I took Mama's old ones. On a sudden inspiration, I put the engagement ring on and ran into the makeup room and flew over to Phil screaming,

"Look what Larry sent me for my birthday!" He just stared at it for half a minute and I think he believed me. Mickey and Ron were there and really believed me. They were so overwhelmingly serious in their congratulations that I became frightened. Had trouble convincing them I was kidding.

4

"A diary makes me think too much"

During the week of September 25, 1959, while Carol Lynn was registering for her junior year, the Russians had aimed a rocket at the moon (an unmanned rocket, to be sure) and had succeeded in planting an 858-pound ball on the surface of the moon itself. Magazines were full of speculation about how soon lunar colonies would be established. Of more interest to Carol Lynn, however, were the glowing reviews given two Broadway actresses – Anne Bancroft and ten-year-old Patty Duke – in a new play, The Miracle Worker. *Her own talent would give Carol Lynn opportunities in the coming year to combine two of her loves: acting and travel – thousands of miles of travel!*

Sep 25, 1959. Registered. Classes are: 2 Education, 2 French, 2 Speech (Stagecraft and Intermediate Acting), and Philosophy.

Sep 27, 1959. Discovered fantastic news: not definite, but very promising that a BYU play (supposedly *Blithe Spirit*) will go on a USO tour of the South Pacific. I've been only undone all day — just can't believe it. I'd give just anything to go!

Oct 5, 1959. Mask Club: Most exciting announcement — the USO trip is for real. Nine weeks of touring Asia. I can't believe it. I've just *got* to go! I want to scream: Ahheeeeeeeeeeeeeeeeeeeeeeeeeeeeeeee!

Oct 9, 1959. Went up to BYU — U of U game (they won). Was hind end of bull for halftime routine — Tom front, Phil matador. Rather fun. Went back to bus and talked. Slept all the way home.

Oct 26, 1959. Can't decide whether Larry has eloped or is in jail — sure it's one of the two.

Nov 13, 1959. Am so excited to have found this old journal to utilize as a diary — do hope it will be as attractive when filled as it is blank.

Nov 18, 1959. Had to go to lecture on dental health tonight. Only thing of interest was the boy on my left who wrote me a note in German asking me to go out with him.

Nov 21, 1959. At last we had tryouts for the play [*Blithe Spirit*]. I read only for Madame Arcati — twice. I sure would love to do it.

Nov 29, 1959. Bob came over and watched a TV program, and then we went to his church. The poor boy is nearly financially bankrupt, and I nearly gagged on the hamburger he bought me. I think it's really a crime that poor scrimping college boys spend money on stupid girls like me who don't even care at all about them.

Dec 2, 1959. Wrote to Larry tonight. I think that thinking about a person becomes very distorted when they're away — especially when you don't correspond regularly.

Dec 3, 1959. Well, two months from now I will be in Japan. I'm on my way. . . . It hasn't really sunk in completely. I just can't believe it!

Dec 5, 1959. Went to game tonight with Bob. Among my conclusions: he is looking for a wife and I don't want to block his view.

Dec 18, 1959. I get to play Madame Arcati! I'm really happy about it — she's one of the best character parts ever written.

Dec 21, 1959. Fred Dixon came up to rehearsal for a while, and we talked for a bit. I really like Fred very much.

Dec 24, 1959. It's only five o'clock in the afternoon, but I'm just resting while my meatloaf is baking, so I thought I'd write a bit. . . . (Later) Fred Dixon came over and made me burn my meatloaf. I think Fred is a very stimulating person.

Jan 1, 1960. I reached quite a decision today that I intend to follow through with. The only thing I can possibly do about Larry is forget him completely. This New Year's resolution is not about to be broken.

Jan 7, 1960. Larry came over for a while this afternoon — very glad he did.

Well, that resolution lasted a week, anyway.

Jan 22, 1960. We're off! We're taking *Blithe Spirit* on a seven-week tour of the Pacific Command, under the direction of the Defense Department. BYU, along with seven other universities in the nation, was selected for this program for entertaining army personnel in Japan, Korea, Okinawa, the Philippine Islands, Guam, Hawaii, and related islands. The group includes: ME as Madame Arcati; Martha Adams — Ruth; Lynne Palmer — Elvira; Margy Potter — Mrs. Bradman; Eleanor Brough — Edith; Harold Oaks — Charles; Phil Keeler — Dr. Bradman; Don Worsley — Dr. Bradman and technician. Dr. Harold I. Hansen is our director, and Mrs. Mayree Reynolds is ladies' chaperone.

Carol Lynn generally takes care to include the complete name of people at least the first time she mentions them in her journals. This is important! You may think you'll never forget who "Bob" or "Kris" is – but as the years pass and the Bobs increase, you may forget. One woman, sorting through a box of pictures, came upon a snapshot she very much wanted to know about. But the only person she recognized was herself. Turning the photo over, she saw some writing on the back. "Good," she said to herself. "Now I can find out who's who, and when this was taken." Then she read what she had written: "The whole gang of us – a week ago Sunday."

Of course, you don't need to write out "Carol Jones" every time you mention her. One way to handle this is to make a list in the back of each year's diary. On a separate page, clearly and fully identify the major characters in that year's book: "Carol Jones – a close friend my own age. Worked with me on the school paper. Later moved to San Francisco." Then, in the journal itself, you can call her "Carol," "CJ," or any nickname you choose, as long as you've identified her in full somewhere and listed the corresponding nickname. Throughout her journals, CLW calls her friend Martha Christensen "Banana" most of the time. What's in a name? Among other things, the key to unlock old memories, so it's worthwhile to keep them straight.

Jan 27, 1960. The flight from Japan to Korea was ghastly. I got so sick I was sure I was going to die immediately. I lost everything I had eaten for four days, and was then taken up to the cockpit for oxygen. I'll never forget sitting on that cold cot with an oxygen mask in one hand and a flight [*airsick*] bag in the other — taking turns until I was dizzy.

Jan 28, 1960. We played here on base. It was freezing cold in the theater, and we had no stage or curtain, as it was actually a service club. It seemed very peculiar to talk to someone on stage and see that his nose was running and red, and frost was rising from his mouth, and then to dash backstage to the gas stove. Our audience seemed really to enjoy the show, however. We had a lot of missionaries and BYU boys there.

Jan 30, 1960. Our performance tonight was at the YWCA in Seoul, and was for the students of Seoul University. The lights went off again during the performance — a most maddening experience. However, the audience still seemed able to follow and enjoy the play.

Jan 31, 1960. We just passed a little funeral procession — people dressed in yellow robes and high hats. Everything is so interesting as we pass by: people with huge bundles on bicycles: boys in school uniforms: children ice skating on ponds: an occasional *papasan* in white robe, tall black hat, and long gray beard; buses packed as only Korean people can pack them; the tiny houses with straw roofs or tile roofs packed so closely together that there almost seems to be no place to walk. The topography of this land appears very similar to that of the United States: jagged mountains in the distance, and hills all over.

Feb 1, 1960. Our performance was at Camp Hovey, about five miles out of Casey, and we had a fairly rowdy audience. We had a lovely big dressing room off left. As I was sneaking around in full costume and makeup, one of the soldiers asked how old I was, and when told that I was twenty, he said, "Ha! She'll never see thirty-five again!"

Feb 4, 1960. Right now we're in the mayor's office; he's at the end of a table and we're all sitting around it. He welcomed us through his translator and gave us each an autographed book, *This Is Seoul*. The mayor is very charming: a globular little man who looked rather lonely in his big, white chair, as we sat around chatting in English. Before we left, he sang us the Korean national song. Then he came down the steps and we took pictures in front of the city hall.

Feb 9, 1960. The show tonight was out of it. We played at six o'clock to a very sparse audience, mostly children. We had a nice big stage, but everything else was in the negative. I instructed Lynne that the next time she has garlic dressing on her salad, she is not to blow in my ear so vehemently: it created chaos all through my system. And if Harold doesn't slap me more gently to wake me from a trance, I'm going to belt him one!

Feb 13, 1960. Our day in Kyoto was fantastic, and I'm only sorry that I can't remember every little detail. . . . [*One highlight was*] the Nijo Imperial Palace, which was in use right up to the last part of the nineteenth century. We had to remove our shoes, of course, and like all these old palaces, it was deathly cold. The floors were all of wood and were called "nightingale floors" because they squeaked in a high key when stepped on. The purpose of this was to prevent surprise assassination attempts on the Shogun (emperor).

CLW obviously got into the spirit of things while traveling, enjoying foreign lands for what they were, and not worrying about what they weren't. If you'd like to read a hilarious "journal" of a person who didn't have this attitude about traveling, I recommend Donald Marshall's short story, "All the Cats in Zanzibar: The Journal of LaRena Homer," in his book, The Rummage Sale.

Feb 21, 1960. We sang hymns all the way home on the bus, and then held a "fireside" here in our room. We all sat around in a cramped circle, while Dr. Hansen talked about his impressions of the Hill Cumorah area and some of the early events there. We all read a favorite scripture, and then ate pie and milk. It was a very satisfying evening, and I'm glad we met.

Feb 22, 1960. Our audience tonight is a group of lion-like Marines. I feel like a bag of peanuts that's gradually being fed to them. On every line that appeals to them, they nearly stand up and hoot, often commenting aloud. When Elvira the ghost told Charles that she doubted he could touch her, and said, "Do you want to?" one bright spectator shouted out, "D___ right!"

Feb 26, 1960. (The Philippines). I was awakened a few minutes ago by the piercing sound of an air-raid siren, and am hoping it's all in the spirit of good fun. From the window above my bed, I thought I saw a strange illumination, but could see nothing but the traffic when I went out onto the porch. I feel like I'm in the midst of a prisoner-of-war camp already; and I can't decide whether to hide under the bed or put some more lotion on my sunburn. I may as well be shot down with a lubricated back, I guess, so on with the lotion and back into bed.

Feb 28, 1960. This afternoon we went out to see the Negrito pygmy village, a short distance out into the wilds. Upon arriving at the gates, we were swamped by natives old and young, trying to sell us blow guns and bows and arrows. Outstanding Personalities We Encoun-

51

tered: (1) A black, elderly little man, wearing nothing but a loincloth, and with a passion for Salem cigarettes. (2) A seventy-five-year-old woman with kinky gray hair, who walked around hugging a plastic raincoat. (3) A sloppily fat woman, nursing a baby and smoking the lighted end of a cigar — occasionally she took it out, shook off the ashes, and began smoking again. (4) Little girls running around in ragged dresses with runny noses and sores on their skin, smoking the lighted ends of cigarettes. (5) Tiny black naked woolly children, playing in the dirt, and utterly charming in their grubbiness.

Mar 3, 1960. Great Scott! Margy just lost her slip *on stage!* Just after the seance, it started slipping down, so she walked behind the sofa, shimmied out of it, and left it there.

(Later that day) Candid Shots Taken with a Mental Brownie Hawkeye: (1) The sunset just as we were leaving the beach. An entire fourth of the sky was a soft yet bright pink, which cast an identical hue on the water. (2) An endless line of little tiny ants, crawling up and down the leg of my bedtable, and carrying away the remains of my coconut shell. (3) Me — lying on the back seat of our bus on the way home, feeling very sad for no particular reason at all. (4) My poor back, still peeling and coming off in great amounts as I showered.

"Candid Shots Taken with a Mental Brownie." CLW discovered a curious surprise more people should find out. A keen sense of observation (which journal-keeping can develop), plus the determination to write things down, can create "mental pictures" that in many ways outdo the finest photographs – even if you never reread the entries. Writing things down fixes the picture in the mind, as well as on paper – another real bonus of journal-keeping.

Mar 4, 1960. I've just finished my second scene, in which Martha, a jet airplane, and I all competed for first place in a sound projection conte.. I think Martha and I tied for second and third.

Mar 9, 1960. I'm so tired I can hardly lift the pen, but since I've been so meticulous in keeping this diary up to this point, I must finish it off in good faith. It is strange to lie here thinking that tomorrow I'll be home picking up my usual life where I left off. And yet, things can never be picked up right where one leaves them when any sustained absence takes place.

Keeping a journal faithfully takes perseverance. Notice how many times CLW is exhausted at the end of a long day of rehearsals or performance, yet

determinedly makes a good entry in her journal before falling into bed. Espe-
cially in the early months, as you start your journal, try not to skip a single
time. After a few months, habit will take over for you. If you do miss a day, or a
week, don't give up; just pick up where you are and go on. Go back and fill in
what you've missed only if you feel like doing so. If you force yourself to
backtrack when you don't want to, you'll get discouraged whenever you skip,
and you will end up not writing at all.

Mar 10, 1960. The event of today for which I am most grateful: Fred
called and asked me to go to the play tomorrow night. We talked for a
long while; Fred is precisely what I need at the moment.

One young mother gave her children the priceless gift of awareness and
zest for life by asking each night as she tucked them in bed one by one: "What
was the most beautiful thing you saw today?" Sometimes she would ask
instead, "the most interesting sound you heard?" or "the nicest thing anyone
did for you?" and so on. You can use such questions occasionally to add
richness to your record.

Mar 17, 1960. Talked to Fred on the phone tonight for about an hour
and discussed many things. One thing was that he wants to do *The Lark*
for his graduate "ism" and cast me as Joan, a part I would dearly love to
do. [*The Lark is a play by Jean Anouilh about Joan of Arc. Carol Lynn's*
portrayals of Joan were to be the epitome of her acting career at BYU.]

Mar 19, 1960. I went out with Fred tonight, and really had a good time.
We saw *Suddenly, Last Summer,* with Katherine Hepburn and Elizabeth
Taylor — a really fine film. After rootbeers and onion rings and running into Selene, we came home and talked in my front room for a
while. Fred is a very nice boy — the kind I ought to fall in love with, but
never will.

Never say "never," Carol Lynn!

Mar 24, 1960. I find that my writing style always appears to be flippant,
which makes it impossible to write about very serious things in a way
that sounds believable.

Mar 31, 1960. Individually Fred and I are fine; as a unit, we're insipid.

Apr 4, 1960. I'm getting sick of licking at the crust of my life and
pretending to myself and everyone else. The world is nothing but a
mass of little selfish ants crawling around senselessly and without
vision. Life is not a clear-cut picture of good and bad. At present, I have

53

no idea of what I am, or what I can have. And I'm afraid I'm no longer a child and I'm as afraid as I have ever been in my life. I'm twenty years old and I can't stand the thought of having to be an adult. I can't think clearly.

I have decided that despite the ideals of unselfish service to humanity, or the rewards of a career, the only way a woman can be happy in life and satisfied to grow older is to be able to live with the person she loves. Perhaps all my fears boil down to this: What happens to those of us who cannot?

Apr 5, 1960. I think that the greatest difficulty of my life is distinguishing honesty from dishonesty in my feelings. Last night I was totally honest in what I wrote, and yet I was fully aware that my feelings would change. And they have — several times.

Apr 6, 1960. Life plays the cruelest games with me — holds a sharp steel blade against my back, only to let me discover that it's really an icicle and is already melting.

Apr 14, 1960. A mad dash to get dinner ready and rush up to the first read-through of *The Lark*. I just love the part — it is beautiful.

Although I'm dead tired, I must write down one significant thought that occurred to me today. I'm sure it was not original, but it was born of my own mind: The worth of the artist has been questioned, and justifiably so, in some ways. But the artist, particularly a combination of the writer and the actor, can do something that the scientist has been trying to do for hundreds of years and will never accomplish. The writer and the actor can actually create life; from their own souls and the elements of the world, they can give birth to a distinct individual who is in many ways more real than those of us who live in the world of "actuality." This is the most thrilling thing I've thought of in a long time.

Apr 20, 1960. I'm wondering at the wisdom of being so completely . . . honest in this diary, as one day someone other than myself might read it. However, I think there's a certain value in it, even if someone who reads this is astounded or puzzled at the picture he draws of the almost-twenty-one-year-old writer. I always wondered how I would feel after first being kissed (off-stage). I thought somehow I would come in the house and cry. I didn't. I laughed.

How honest should we be in a journal? How frank? My suggestion is that

54

we should be strictly honest as concerns ourselves and strictly merciful as concerns others. After all, a journal is essentially our *story. We know our own thoughts, feelings, and, usually, motivations – good and bad. An honest journal should reflect a balanced view of the real person, as nearly as we can portray it. Half of the vigor and value of a diary are lost if we record only the "up" moments, only our nobler sentiments.*

On the other hand, since we do not *know the hearts and inner feelings of others, we should go easy on heavy condemnations of them, and especially on criticisms based only on hearsay and gossip. That does not mean we need to falsify our feelings about people, or leave such reactions out of our journals: we just need to distinguish between personal response and objective truth.*

Apr 26, 1960. After rehearsal, Larry and I went down to his apartment and cooked supper. He read me two scenes from his play — quite good. Also he read me things from his journal — which he said he had never done before. There were some excellent things in it, and I feel like I know Larry a great deal better. One thing he wrote about me was the last night I saw him before I left on tour: "Carol Lynn is one of the few women I've known whom I admire completely." — a compliment I would have traded for the slightest word of subjective affection.

May 2, 1960. I sort of hate to close this day. It's one of those times when I'd like to stay awake forever and just be here, living on what just happened.

Playing Joan of Arc on stage tonight was one of the truly satisfying and thrilling moments of my life. It was an honest performance, also; the emotions I felt were not for me, they were for Joan, and when I cried, the tears were not mine, they were hers. I loved every minute of it, and I felt closer to myself, to the world, and to God than I think I ever have.

May 3, 1960. The only two goals in life I care about at present are those of making myself into a real and sensitive artist and making myself into a real and complete woman. I could not say that these conflict, but I do know that the closer I get to realizing myself as an artist-person, the further I get from my goal of being a woman. I suppose one cannot see oneself clearly, but about myself I do know this much: I am not a *woman*, I am a *person*. But this I also know: that if being a *woman* means giving up one fraction of what I am as a person, I can never do it. It may sound too dramatic to quote from Joan, but the words, "What I am I will not denounce" have a definite meaning for me. I feel a great compulsion not to disavow my real self, even though often I dislike myself for it.

I am very grateful to Fred for thinking of me primarily as a woman instead of a person. Very few boys have done this. I have a tremendous talent for being a good friend.

May 8, 1960. Today is Mother's Day, and it passed much as usual. I wonder sometimes why I am so devoid of the maternal instinct. As a rule, women are supposed to be filled with a passionate yearning to have and rear children. I can look at babies and think how interesting and charming they are, but never once do I recall having even a fleeting desire to have one of my own.

May 14, 1960. Anyway, I'm going to persevere in hunting for Fred's ultimate reality. If ever found, the results might be amazing. Aside from that, I'm thoroughly enjoying the process — thoroughly.

May 24, 1960. I believe perhaps Tom is getting a bit romantic in his dotage. I got a letter from him today, written on bright blue paper to "match my eyes while I read it."

Jun 11, 1960. In some ways tonight was very good. I feel a lot closer to Fred than I used to, although we still don't communicate — really. I think that probably I puzzle Fred a good deal. He may still go to New York; as a matter of fact, I hope he doesn't.

Jun 13, 1960. I started my student teaching experience this morning — we have three classes of children's theater, and I really think I will enjoy them.

Jun 15, 1960. After rehearsal, Fred came over, and we celebrated his birthday by watching television, drinking lemonade, burning incense and a candle (and the carpet), and setting off sparklers on my patio out back.

Jun 19, 1960. I wish I could write down some profound things about Fred: he's leaving in the morning for New York. Even if I should never see or hear from Fred again, I will count him as an important factor in my young life — and one for which I am unexpressibly grateful.

Jun 24, 1960. The play opened tonight and went quite well, I think. I feel quite good about what I did [*Laura in* The Glass Menagerie].

Jul 2, 1960. I read two plays this evening and half of another — *The*

Four-Poster and *Here Come the Clowns*. I'm halfway through *Anna Christie* by O'Neill. I had hoped to hear from Fred today, but I didn't. I was perfectly aware that his absence would make my heart grow fonder, and it has.

Jul 3, 1960. The major event of the day was my writing a poem — a rather long and totally different theme than I've ever tried. I'm not sure, but I think I like it. The title is, "And She Shall Be Called Woman." The last few lines I will record here (also the introduction):

> Introduction:
> Eve, Mother of All, a prayer to thee.
> All else to God, but this to thee,
> For thou art woman.

> Last stanza:
> Mother, tell me what to do.
> All other prayers to God,
> But this to thee, for
> Thou hast been a woman, for so long.
> Help me, Eve — Mother of All.

Jul 12, 1960. This evening I rewrote my poem, "She Shall Be Called Woman." Probably it is the best thing I've written — at least it is the most honest without being overly saturated with uncontrolled emotion. It concerns something very near to me about which I have been quite disturbed for years: the place of woman in the universe as related to both God and man. I've read every scripture that exists in all four of the standard works.... Were those spirits who were designated "women" so designated because as original intelligences they were somehow lesser to those designated "men"?

Jul 16, 1960. We rehearsed [*Clinton Larson's* Mantle of the Prophet] morning and evening with the afternoon off. It's a very complicated lighting plot, and if I hadn't had Ron Olauson there I would have gone to pieces [*CLW was doing lights*]. I am so inefficient mechanically that the most difficult task they dared give me is that of cutting seven-inch square jells of "surprise pink" and "chocolate" on the paper cutter.

Jul 23, 1960. Tom came over today to iron a shirt and then came with me to get groceries and to the library. I really think I've succeeded in establishing our relationship on the casual level that I think it's got to be on to survive. Very soon I'm sure he'll forget he ever had any serious ideas about me at all.

Jul 26, 1960. Suddenly it has occurred to me that in fifty years when someone reads this, they will not have any idea at all of the appearance of the main characters. I will therefore attempt to give a slight description of myself and the three gentlemen featured herein.

Me: This is a somewhat difficult proposition. I am 5'6" tall and weigh 117 pounds. I have always felt conspicuously underweight, but perhaps that is not so. My unglamorous measurements are 34-24-34. My hair (brown, already sprinkled generously with pure white) is now comparatively long, and I wear it at present in a bouffant pageboy. At my best I look "pleasant" or "interesting," never approaching the beautiful. Among all my physical features, however, I do possess one thing that saves me from hopeless unattractiveness: my eyes. They are wide set, of a very deep blue, with extremely long and dark lashes. And that is a sufficient summary of the author.

Such word-pictures will be most helpful to future readers of your journals (including yourself!), and, in addition, it's excellent practice for the aspiring writer. Give it a try!

Jul 27, 1960. I have discovered what I consider a much more noble means of prayer than kneeling at a bedside. That is in the open night, gazing into heaven with eyes open. I am not here referring to effective communication with nature. I refer to the most actual and intimate conversation with God that is possible. I wish I could sometime have the words to describe the glory and satisfaction of true prayer. True prayer, I think, is very rare, even in those of us who conscientiously apply this principle. In all my weaknesses and falseness, however, I have come close enough to realize its significance. Only through prayer and acting have I ever approached the self-fulfillment searched for by every sensitive person.

Aug 1, 1960. My Church history class always upsets me because I see so clearly that I'm doing so little with my life in every way. Right now I can see six or seven different directions in which I could pour my entire life's energy, and I've really no idea which pursuit is most valuable. My only salvation seems to be to live from day to petty day in a sort of suspension. But I know that this "suspension" or lack of initiative is the most damning thing in human progress.

Aug 5, 1960. Today I took ten of my poems to school and read them to Mr. Golightly. In general, he seemed to like them very much — and I don't think that he was merely being kind. I'd love to think that I had the ability to someday write really good things.

Aug 7, 1960. For experimental purposes, I just wrote a triolet.

Triolet

The seasons come, the seasons go,
And love is yet a-hiding.
While Cupid bends his willow bow,
The seasons come, the seasons go.
While Venus in her gardens low
Exhales an amorous tiding,
The seasons come, the seasons go,
And love is yet a-hiding.

Aug 10, 1960. Fred must be losing his mind or something. I came home at noon to find three letters from him.

Aug 16, 1960. I've concluded that it's quite true that I frighten men. All who heard me speak were duly impressed, but woe to the woman who gives the impression of being an efficient intellect or an accomplished scholar. I wonder what Fred sees in me?

Aug 24, 1960. Finally got a letter from Fred today: very short and dull. I think I ought to start forgetting Fred entirely.

Aug 25, 1960. However, I'm afraid that I won't.

Aug 31, 1960. Perhaps I shouldn't keep a diary. It makes me think too much. It might not show by the things I write down, but nonetheless it is true — and quite dangerous for a woman, especially a woman like me.

Yes, a journal does make you think – another of its bonuses. As for "dangerous," well, someone said: "Ye shall know the truth, and the truth shall make you free, but first it shall make you hurt." Whoever made that statement was wise indeed. Those who value truth feel it's worth the price.

"Sing of
her divine origin"

In the fall of 1960 the presidential campaign captured massive headlines, with John F. Kennedy and Richard M. Nixon running a close and heated race. In the 1960 Olympics, Wilma Rudolph, a young black woman who had been unable to walk until she was eight, earned three gold medals in track. And fall fashion news raved about a "brand new breed of knits" that was revolutionizing the textile industry. The new fabric, virtually wrinkleproof, would herald an era in which women no longer had to spend hours over the ironing board. For a young college student with the crammed, hectic schedule Carol Lynn had, such an invention was a blessing indeed.

Sep 20, 1960. Something came into my life today that might very well result in something significant. Dave Jacobs, Culture Office vice-president, and Maria Toronto, his assistant, came to my home and asked me to write and direct the Central Assembly Committee assembly, which will be held October 21. They want the assembly to be a tribute to President David O. McKay, with the hope of his being there at its presentation.

I spent all afternoon and evening reading President McKay's biography, sketches and tributes by various people, and the entire book by his secretary, Clare Middlemiss — *Cherished Memories.*

Sep 26, 1960. A short while ago as I was staring at my ceiling, I spotted the spider which has eluded me for two weeks. I rushed for the vacuum, and immediately the poor creature was sucked to his death.

Sep 27, 1960. As of today, I am twenty-one years of age. I just finished reading the letter I wrote to myself in my last year's diary at this time. I would answer it, but that writer is long since dead. I do, however, want to write to myself of next year at this time.

Dear Twenty-two:

How frightening it is to write that figure: it seems so enormous! Perhaps you aren't as afraid of maturity as I am, but in all truthfulness, a sort of shudder runs through me as I realize that now, at twenty-one, I am considered a completely mature adult. I think that in many ways I am an adult, but in so many other ways I'm still a child. And I don't want to grow up! Just as passionately as Peter Pan, I say I want always to be young and to have fun!

So much has happened to me within this past year! Of course, spending seven weeks in Asia was rather an unlooked-for event. Writing *The Hunter* was something I still am quite proud of. I've done some good acting this past year, too: Madame Arcati, Laura, but especially Joan! I've kept my grade-point average above 3.8, for what-ever that means. I've read quite a bit, and written a few things that are fairly good.

But inside — my feelings, attitudes, etc., have undergone perhaps the most notable evolution. If as many things happen next year as have in the past one, I might scarcely recognize myself. I know that there are many vital decisions that have to be made. Perhaps you will be teaching school somewhere, Twenty-two; maybe you will be doing graduate studies. You might even have been called to fulfill a mission for the Church — and you could even be married!

By this time next year, you'll have had to decide essentially what will happen to you for the remainder of your life. I am not really fearful for you, if only you will think *honestly* and stay close to God.

The one thing you have got to do next year — before anything significant can happen — is to discover why you are a woman. If I would beg anything of you, it is this: *please* make that discovery the most important single discovery you try to make. *I* don't know the answer; I hope in one year, *you* will know.

Love,
CLW at Twenty-one.

Oct 3, 1960. Got a letter from Phil today. He had addressed it to "Mrs. Magnolia Jones," and Daddy spent the whole noon hour chasing around the block to find a "Mrs. Magnolia Jones." [*"Magnolia" and "Jazbo" were CLW's and Larry's nicknames for each other.*]

Oct 8, 1960. I have *got* to play Anne Frank!

Oct 10, 1960. I swear, I *swear*, that I don't know what it is about me that makes boys forget that I am of the opposite sex.

Oct 13, 1960. Today I spoke with President McKay in his office. . . . The main problem that pertains to the assembly is the health of his wife, who has been quite ill and has had several strokes. He plans to take her to California next week and so would be gone on the 21st. He said that without her presence, he didn't even feel that he could come, and added that she is responsible for whatever his life has amounted to. I was very impressed by the way in which he spoke of his wife.

Our plans for the assembly are now to postpone it to a future date with the hope of Sister McKay being able to attend with President McKay. He was very gracious to us and expressed appreciation for our coming. He looked very tired and somewhat older than I thought he might look. It was really a thrill to meet him, and I will always remember it.

Oct 31, 1960. At 11:30 P.M., as I was undressing, the phone rang. It was Morris Sargent, ward-teaching supervisor, who told me that I was the only one in the ward who had not been visited. They wanted a 100 percent record, and the deadline was only a few minutes away, so he asked if he could come over for a brief lesson. Of course, I consented, put on my bathrobe, and had the shortest and most peculiar ward-teaching visit I've ever had.

Nov 2, 1960. A very good thing happened to me today: Dr. Woodbury cast me as Regan in *King Lear*.

Nov 5, 1960. On the way home from seeing *Our Town* in Salt Lake today, Dave Jacobs mentioned that his great-grandfather crossed the plains seven times. To which I replied: "Couldn't make up his mind, hum?"

Nov 7, 1960. Our President McKay assembly will be held on the 18th of this month. He will not be here: Sister McKay is so ill that he leaves her only when it's imperative.

Nov 9, 1960. The further I progress in life, the more sure I am of one thing: the only way I can lead a satisfying life — that is, one opposed to desperation and despair — is to establish such a real and living relationship with God that I can ascribe the complete guidance of my life to His care.

Nov 18, 1960. All things considered, I would say the assembly was most definitely a success. A large crowd was there (four to five thousand), the cast created the kind of atmosphere I'd hoped, and the effect on the audience seemed to be almost remarkable. At the time we present the scroll with student signatures to President McKay (maybe on Wednesday), we will also give him a tape of the assembly, which his children said they would like to play for the McKay Thanksgiving celebration. It seems impossible for me to realize that something I've created — primarily with my own efforts — could find its way into the Thanksgiving celebration of President McKay and his family.

Nov 20, 1960. It may be all in my mind, but I have a feeling that if Fred were here, I would find new things in him as well as in myself.

Dec 2, 1960. Tom keeps talking about my going to California with him for Christmas. I'm sure I won't.

Dec 7, 1960. Fred is a very normal, well-adjusted individual who needs a normal, well-adjusted wife. This certainly eliminates me, I think!

Dec 8, 1960. Our second performance of *King Lear* is over and I feel quite good about it. I wish I could explain what a thrilling thing it is to act! During those moments when I am on the stage, the entire world assumes an order — even if it is somewhat disorderly within the framework of the play — that I find nowhere else. Life becomes synthesized, emotion purified, compressed, and directionalized.

Dec 18, 1960. Sometimes I like myself tremendously and other times I feel a great distaste for myself. Why?

Dec 19, 1960. I have just left Fred, and I don't know what to write. Nothing has radically changed. I'm sure we're much closer than we were before, but still I feel tremendously alone. Things aren't like they should be, and I'm not like I should be, and Fred's not like he should be.

Dec 21, 1960. 7:10 P.M. I wonder sometimes if I ought not to burn my diaries and never write another word. It's almost an obsession with me to painfully peel off my emotions and spread them onto a sheet of paper.

Dec 22, 1960. Today is my mother's birthday. I feel more than ever before the loss that is mine in not having a mother. I wish I could talk to someone whom I knew loved me — as I'm sure she would, in spite of myself.

Dec 26, 1960. I'm writing this sitting in the little old rocker given to me by my mother when I was eight, as it had been given to her when she was eight. At present, I am nurturing a calmness and an optimism within my breast that I intend most earnestly to cultivate.

Jan 5, 1961. Why am I always so quick to underestimate myself? Am I really and truly a full-fledged masochist? God help me! I think I *try* to be honest, but maybe I live in an entire world of self-deception. I think I'm improving. Tonight was a big step forward.

Jan 7, 1961. Now I want to report something that is of great satisfaction to me: I find that I can now pray more successfully than I've been able to for a long time. God must indeed be very patient! As I've tried to explain, I cannot possibly live my life sanely if I believe that the very important matters of my life are governed by mere chance, or even by human discretion. Most truly, I do believe that God can and will determine one's experiences and opportunities to the extent that complete trust in Him is developed and His will invoked.

Jan 9, 1961. It would seem that I've been rejected as a possible Anne Frank.

Jan 17, 1961. How I admire people who can write poetry, and how I love to read it and recite it!

Jan 19, 1961. I swear, I vow, and I promise that someday I am going to write a poem that is not only passable as a reasonably well-expressed thought, but actually a fine piece of writing. Someday!

Feb 2, 1961. Tom and I are wonderful. I marvel at us every time I think about it.

Feb 9, 1961. Tonight Fred and I saw a very poor movie: *Teahouse of the August Moon*. It was so bad that we left and watched "Twilight Zone" on TV here. I now find that I feel thoroughly comfortable with Fred. This is such a very different and new experience for me that I see whole new vistas of life opening for my exploration.

Feb 11, 1961. Hearts that go barefoot get their toes stepped on. . . . I hope that I will be able to pray tonight. (Later) Writing always calms me, I think. Putting my passions into written form at least makes me feel a sense of productivity about my pains.

"How can I know what I mean," said one little girl, *"until I see what I've said?"* Beyond question, writing gives order and understanding to our thoughts, as CLW expresses here when she says it *"calms"* her. Writing also generates, brings about, *other thoughts and understandings that we never would have without the writing – it helps us "know what we mean" in the deepest part of ourselves. It leads us to the prize of self-knowledge.*

Feb 16, 1961. I keep forgetting to mention my valentine from Tom. He came knocking on my bedroom window at 1:30 Valentine's night, and presented me with a huge, three-foot heart that he had made at the Scene Shop and covered with red satin. On it was written:

> Carol Lynn,
>   This late eve
>   I give thee
>   This heart of
>   Staples, satin,
>   And soiled tears.
>   Love, Tom

Feb 23, 1961. Margy Potter and I are staying tonight with my Uncle Warren and Aunt Arvilla Sirrine here in Dingle, Idaho. Our first tour stop [*Blithe Spirit*] was Montpelier, and the show went rather well, considering all that might easily have gone wrong.

There's something comforting and secure about the clean sheets, frilly curtains, noisy furnace, and carefully arranged knick-knacks in the home of a relative — especially if the house is semi-isolated off the main road of a little town called "Dingle Dell."

Mar 1, 1961. I feel like I want to write something about Fred, but I am rather unsure of what's happening. We sit together on the bus all the time and eat together also. I do not feel impressed that we're building for something great in the future; but I do feel that we are temporarily sharing something good. And for me, that is a most valuable experience.

Mar 7, 1961. In Senior Seminar today we had a ridiculous free-for-all debate on "Resolved: that women should support men while men support culture." Needless to say, I was right there in the middle of it.

Before I left on tour, I gave Dr. Clinton Larson most of my poems to read; and today I went in to talk to him about them. He said that I am very sensitive, have much talent, but need to be more courageous in my writing.

Mar 9, 1961. All evening, I've been at tryouts for *J. B.* I'm almost afraid to put down how I feel; I read several times for Sarah, J. B.'s wife. I would love to play this part! This will be the first amateur release of the play, and being in it would be such a thrill! Well, "the Lord giveth and the Lord taketh away."

Mar 11, 1961. "The Lord giveth! Blessed be the name of the Lord!" I am going to play the part of Sarah! And it is nothing less than a miracle how completely the play explores the very thing that especially lately has bothered me so tremendously: keeping a faith in God when there is no rational basis for that faith, and living life because it exists — loving because it is the only answer to being.

Mar 15, 1961. I didn't write last night: it would have been anticlimactic after an evening of Fred and The Rain. (I meant that to sound romantic, not soggy.) We went to see *Kiss Me, Kate,* and then out to eat tacos. Things were really very, very good, I think. I still can't define what's happening to me: I feel like I've been whitewashed inside and there's a breeze blowing on the still-wet paint. This imagery may be ludicrous, but it conveys the sensation.

Mar 25, 1961. Again I failed to write: not Fred and The Rain — Fred and The Snow.

Mar 31, 1961. The one thing in this world that I am certain of is that the entirety of both my sanity and my happiness is dependent upon the clarity and the intensity of my relationship with God. To me this means being at peace with every element of my life in a recognition of God's guidance. For the past several weeks, I have felt at home in the world, emotionally relaxed, and somewhat secure in myself. This condition has, I believe, brought me closer to God regarding my state of mind, but in another way, it has somewhat cut me off. I have not felt such a tremendous need for intense prayer — perhaps I should say "desperate" prayer. For some time now my praying habits have been somewhat haphazard, to say the least. It's not that each evening at prayer time I would smugly disregard the need to articulate my thoughts; perhaps I have felt that the very fact of finding happiness in life is sort of a prayer itself. It almost seems sufficient for me to form a single thought as I fall asleep: "You're right, God — life is good." But this is not enough! And it is so easy to lose God!

There is nothing — nothing — nothing in this world that is consistently reliable except God — and He is reliable only to the degree that we cultivate a strong and enduring relationship with Him.

Apr 2, 1961. Easter Sunday. All resurrection need not wait until after one is dead.

Dear, sweet Tom! He is truly a choice spirit, and I love him dearly. We sat in the swings across the street for a long time and talked about many things that we never had even mentioned before. I even asked for his reaction to Fred and me as a combination. Tom is so perceptive and so sensitive to my feelings that it's almost uncanny. I hadn't realized that he watches me so closely.

Apr 3, 1961. Picture this: Me, searching in my purse for my inhaler, diligently applying it to each nostril — only to discover that in my hand, instead of the inhaler, was a tube of pink lipstick!

Apr 4, 1961. Prayer both morning and evening makes the day so secure and orderly — like a neatly sliced piece of time pressed into a spiritual sandwich.

Apr 6, 1961. Before I begin today's account, let me just mention that I have been awarded a $1,250 fellowship for graduate study here next year.

Apr 9, 1961. God is so generous and patient that I almost must despise myself for my lack of faith. I needn't hold my breath for fear the universe will topple if I don't hold it together by diligent worry. "God's in his heaven, all's right with the world," said Robert Browning.

Apr 12, 1961. I must mention that today the Soviets announced the return of their first spaceman. Rather a landmark in history.

Apr 19, 1961. Inside of me there is a strange combination of exuberance and solemnity. I don't know if it would ever be possible to describe what it is to act on the stage. Perhaps one day I will try. All I will say now is that existence somehow sifts itself and becomes intensely beautiful — sort of like what sometimes happens in prayer.

Apr 21, 1961. Lately Fred and I are quite on the top of our ferris-wheel cycle. Perhaps if I don't think about the ride down it won't be so

67

noticeable — just a slight rush of wind in the face and that queasy feeling in the stomach.

Apr 30, 1961. "Be loved, not because we are anxious to be loved, but because we are worthy to be loved." This is the message I got from stake conference today, in which Elder Hanks spoke. This motto would be appropriate emblazoned on my ceiling, or tattooed upon my hand.

May 1, 1961. Sometimes it helps to receive comfort from others, but giving comfort is a much more healing project.

May 5, 1961. Nearly always, after I have left Fred, I feel a sort of sinking in the stomach that makes me want to run back and complete something quite indefinable that forever remains uncompleted.

Have you noticed that by this time, CLW is getting much better at expressing even the hard-to-define feelings?

May 9, 1961. Tom came by a short while ago, scratching at my window screen and presenting me with flowers he had picked on his way home from the library. I am going to miss him so very much!

May 10, 1961. Our Finnish lecturer spoke in directing class this afternoon. She discussed the responsibilities of Americans toward world peace. At times like this I feel such a fierce dedication to do something wonderful! Why do people want to hide behind the sleazy curtain of "modesty" whenever they are approached with the frightening possibility of doing anything significant? I really don't know what kind of a contribution I am supposed to make, but I fully intend to do *something*!

May 14, 1961. Today is Mother's Day, and there is no more appropriate time to make the introduction of my stepmother-to-be. Daddy and Gladys Broulin, a widow in the ward, have decided to marry at the end of June. I think I feel good about the whole thing.

May 18, 1961. Fred took his orals today and passed them. He called this afternoon to let me know how they went. I try not to think about Fred; I'm sort of emotionally marking time until we separate.

May 21, 1961. The funniest thing I've heard all year: Joan of Arc's dying words — "Yes, I'm smoking more now but enjoying it less!"
As I was eating my before-bedtime snack, Tom came over, and we

ate and giggled for an hour. This time he brought me snowballs and tulips, now properly placed on my bedtable.

May 25, 1961. For how many years now have I coveted the BYU "Best Actress" award? Well, tonight that trophy is sitting on my bookcase. I am indeed very pleased and grateful for it.

Jun 1, 1961. As I put on my cap and gown this evening for baccalaureate services, my image in the mirror seemed exactly as I remember me in my *high school* graduation gown. It's not fair to have to live in the same physical structure when there have been at least a dozen deaths and resurrections inside me.

Today I wrote little letters of appreciation to many of those who have contributed significantly to my college career: Drs. Hansen, Woodbury, Mitchell, Clinger, Gledhill, the Pardoes, and Bishop Fletcher.

June 8, 1961. Yesterday Tom came up from Salt Lake to see me, and I spent all of today in Salt Lake with him. The zoo was much fun; we wandered around eating, chatting with the monkeys, and casting snide remarks at the shedding camel. Then, sitting by the geranium bed and the duck pond, we made a solemn pact, written and signed by both of us, that in exactly ten years at 1 P.M., we would meet at that exact spot. I intend to be there.

Do you ever wonder how such "we'll-meet-here-in-ten-years" pacts turn out? Here's what happened in this instance: Carol Lynn writes, "On June 8, 1971, with husband, two children, and baby in my womb, I went to the zoo and sat by the duck pond. Tom did not come."

Jun 11, 1961. Written late last night.

Exorcism

> If I could place a tea-cup over each
> Cricket that calls from the tall grass. . . .
> If I could blow out the stars, one by one,
> And then peel the moon from the sky. . . .
> If I could cast the scented breeze into
> A great well on the other side of the mountain. . . .
> Perhaps then I could walk into
> The night without you still beside me.

Jun 15, 1961. Today was Fred's birthday, and I gave him two books: the works of Robert Browning, and *Sonnets from the Portuguese and Other Love Poems* by E. B. Browning. After we ate, I read some of the sonnets to him; that particular few minutes of time is now shelved with my "Moments of Great Beauty to Remember."

Jun 17, 1961. I've been reading in Isaiah tonight. What marvelous poetry the Bible contains!

Jun 21, 1961. I don't think Fred knows how very hard his leaving is going to be for me. And, in spite of everything, I don't believe it will be entirely easy for him to erase me from his life, either. But I suspect that he has gone through this sort of thing so often that it holds little of the uniqueness that it holds for me. I am so selfish. And yet beyond that, I do so want Fred to be happy that I think I can be content to sever our lives if that is what is necessary.

Jun 22, 1961.

Occupation

I think that all
I shall do today
Is sit on this
Stool in front of

      The big clock and
      Pinch each lazy
      Minute as it
      Strolls by, hoping

            To more quickly
            Bring the sun
            To the mountain
            And you to me.

Jun 29, 1961. I'm still in the world, and the world is still lovely.

Jun 30, 1961. I'm still in the world, but the world seems not quite so beautiful.

Ten minutes ago I left Fred for the last time — at least for a long while; maybe forever. Our farewells were not eloquent. What can be said when there are a hundred thoughts that words cannot touch, just floating in the air?

Jul 2, 1961. The policy of fasting once a month is a wise one, I think. How very much easier it makes feeling close to God — realizing complete dependence on him. Not often do I bear my testimony in Church, but I did this morning. I hadn't planned on it at all, but I suddenly felt that I should. I felt so good inside about many things in general and a few in particular.

Jul 5, 1961. I shall be interested to learn — at that great millennial panorama of history — if Ernest Hemingway really did kill himself. Suicide is something that I can comprehend to a certain degree because of psychological climates I've gone through. But right now I'm most happy to report that I am quite satisfied with living. My present days are pleasant and peaceful. I can smile at myself in the mirror; and when — in the night time — I reach out and touch my own hand, I feel friendly towards it.

Jul 16, 1961. Living in a body is often rather cumbersome and annoying, but also it's quite pleasant to exist in matter. I mean, it's exciting to easily manipulate one's arms and legs, to brush one's hair vigorously, to sneeze, or to feel a sunburn.

Of sheer fatigue, I slept in this morning and missed Sunday School — an almost unprecedented event in my young life.

Jul 23, 1961. I have found it tremendously disturbing to get so far behind in this diary. Perhaps I've become a sort of slave to it; but truly I feel a sort of disorder in my life unless I impose a certain order by keeping a fairly strict account in writing. Now I can sleep more peacefully.

Jul 31, 1961. This evening I began a most significant experience in my life; I am reading *Women of Mormondom* by Edward W. Tullidge, written for and about the women of this last dispensation. I must record my first impression upon opening the book. I skimmed over a few comments, and then lighted upon this paragraph on p. 177: "Presently woman herself shall sing of her divine origin. A high-priestess of the faith shall interpret the themes of herself and of her Father-and-Mother God!"

The most glorious dream that I have ever dared to let play upon my consciousness is that of, in some way, discovering and singing the divine existence of woman. I have no way of knowing whether or not God has given me the capacity even to approach this dream, or whether I am personally worthy to make the attempt. All I know is that my soul cries out almost audibly — with an overpowering desire both to experience and to reclaim the rightful fulfillment of woman's cre-

71

ation. . . . Whether or not I bear the potential of being a "high priestess" able to sing the themes of womanhood and my "Father-and-Mother God" to ears other than my own — at least I shall sing them to myself.

Those of you who know Carol Lynn's work will see the path from this experience to several of her books – particularly Daughters of Light *and* The Flight and the Nest *– and many of her poems.*

Aug 3, 1961. Yesterday I got a letter from Fred. He is enjoying New York tremendously.

Aug 8, 1961. As I was cutting tomatoes for a salad this evening, something wonderful occurred to me. Before I came down to this earth, I had somewhat of a knowledge of what was going to happen to me. I had a clearer view of the plan of existence and knew my place in it. And with this knowledge, I consented to come here!

I was a rational, perceptive being. I must have looked upon the Plan with acceptance and satisfaction; I must have found my place in this whole pattern desirable. Otherwise, I would never have consented to come here.

This is marvelously comforting to me. I once knew the pattern of existence — and accepted it. Surely I can trust my own judgment, although it was made at a time I cannot now recall.

Aug 26, 1961. There was a very sweet letter from Fred. Besides working for Mr. Wanamaker, he is secretary to the actress Tammy Grimes. He is tremendously busy and seems to be happy.

Sep 3, 1961.

Haiku

The midnight rain salts
The silence of my slumber
And I wake to hear

It drop on the tin
Of my roof with the sound of
A thousand kisses.

Sep 5, 1961. Today I learned something that virtually sent me into a frenzy of delight. The spring production will be *The Lark* by Anouilh. I can scarcely believe it. All day long I have felt like running or screaming. Today I said to Dr. Hansen, "Dr. Hansen, if you let someone else play Joan, *she'd better be good!*" I have *got* to play Joan. I have GOT to.

Sep 13, 1961. Last night was my first rehearsal for *Arsenic and Old Lace*, and I've got only three more before we open.

Sep 19, 1961. Opening night. It really is a fun play to do, and I feel quite good about it.

Sep 20, 1961. I had a lengthy conversation with Dr. Clinton Larson about my major problem — and I think I gained a great deal from it. "Forget it," he told me. "Push from your mind all ideas that are unappealing. It is impossible that you will ever be brought to a situation that your nature cannot accept."

He thinks that by no means is woman an inferior creation, that man's "authority" is an illusion — that he is forced to deal largely with things that are utter nonsense, whereas woman is allowed to deal with reality and truth because of the nature of her being. The office of man — including his authority, accomplishments, priesthood, etc. — is largely one of "mending the fences."

"Am I just a twenty-two-year-old failure?"

The 1960s would be a decade of great change for the United States. Patterns of life shifted on every front: political, social, moral, military, racial, cultural – choose what you will. Americans did a turnabout in little things as well as big. For example, in the late fifties, BYU President Ernest L. Wilkinson tried to persuade students to ride bicycles to the Provo campus instead of taxing the limited parking space with their thousands of cars. But bicycles weren't fashionable in the fifties, and few students complied. A decade later, the problem would be finding enough places to park the bikes, because bicycling would be "in."

During the week of September 27, 1961, when this chapter opens, Life magazine reported on another sporting fad: surfing. "Surfing, just beginning to catch on around the rest of the U. S., has become an established craze in California." Happily for Carol Lynn, there was no surf in Utah; as a busy graduate student studying, acting, working on her master's thesis, and keeping up her end of a New York-Provo romance, she would have had no time for such a craze – established or otherwise!

Sep 27, 1961. As is my custom, I have just finished scanning my diaries and reading the letter I wrote a year ago to myself of today. And to keep up the tradition, I shall make my contribution to next year's reader:

Dear Twenty-three:

I think that I would first like to make my annual report on the significant things of the year — with the speculations of Twenty-one in mind.

THINGS I HAVE DONE — I have done some good acting: Regan, Sarah, Abby. My life would be so different without the benefit of acting — so unutterably dull!

I have written some things of merit — many poems that I am proud of, three studentbody assemblies, and my play adaptation. I have read a great deal — plays, poetry, Church books. I graduated from college with a B. S. in Theater and a minor in English. I was on the high honor roll with a 3.84 grade-point average.

I am not proud of everything I have done or been this last year. Many things that have occurred, especially within me, I am regretful for. . . . The only watchword to life is FAITH!

Speculations for next year? I want to play Joan! I want to like myself more of the time. I want to be closer to God and to harbor no alienating feelings in my heart. I want to write, I want to act, but most of all, I want to live: TO BE!

> With a toast for the future
> And a tear for the past,
>
> Carol Lynn, 1961.

Here we see how the yearly birthday letter has progressed to become both evaluation of the past and challenge for the future. If you are interested in such an annual accounting, whether on your birthday or at year's end, or another time, here are some ways to use your journal to help you survey the past and plan for the future. You probably would not want to use all of the following questions in your letter or evaluation; one or two might be all you'd need at a time. But ask yourself:

— What can I do now that I couldn't do a year ago? (Play tennis, read French, run a mile, make a tailored suit, understand challenging poetry, and so on.)

— Whom do I count as good friends now that I was not close to (or even aware of) twelve months ago?

— What especially significant prayers have been answered?

— What new habits have I developed this year? (Visiting the sick on Sundays, exercising daily, regular scripture study, avoiding gossip, writing faithfully in my journal, and so forth.)

— What kind of a steward have I been over my material possessions? (Painted the back fence, enlarged the vegetable garden, repaired cracked plaster, faithfully had car maintained, added $200 to savings account, passed on discarded clothing items to those who could use them, and so on.)

75

Of course, each of these questions applies to the past. By skimming through your journal, you will find answers – perhaps pleasantly surprising ones. Then, if you wish, turn the questions toward the future: What do I want to do in a year that I can't do now? Whom do I want to know better? What new habits do I want to work on? Write the questions down, and, in a year, have an accounting!

Oct 3, 1961. The mountains are indescribably beautiful in their autumn colors. And lately, in the evenings, I feel a certain — what? — nostalgia creep about me. Last night I sat in my living room in the dark, watching the church lights across the street, and driving my loneliness like a nail into a soft board.

Oct 11, 1961. Elder Kimball spoke in Devotional today on prayer. It was a very fine discourse.

Lately I have been employing a most rewarding device regarding prayer: writing in my diary and praying *in the living room*. If I'm in bed when I write in my diary, it's so easy to stay there and sneak by with a third-rate prayer. But if I don't go in to my bedroom until I'm ready to sleep, I can discipline myself more easily.

Notice the interesting relationship here between Carol Lynn's diary writing and her prayers. Obviously, her pattern was to make her journal entry, then pray. The meditation and self-examination involved in writing surely formed the basis for her prayer and personal report to her Father; the two together seem to have formed an on-going process of repentance, goal-setting, evaluation, planning, more goal-setting, and so forth. Each activity strengthened the other.

Oct 12, 1961. What excellent fun to write while soaking in the bathtub, contemplating the day and letting a tiny stream of water drops trickle onto my foot.

This evening I began my research on my "pilot study" — finding materials in Church history suitable for comedy dramatization. It's hard to know where to begin. I'd love to read through some of the old diaries. And I get sidetracked so often that I fear it shall take me forever to exhaust even a few resources.

Oct 19, 1961. I discovered a most exciting thing today! I'm compiling the *Sand in Their Shoes* scrapbook; and inside the front cover of the souvenir program is a poem by my great-great-grandfather, Thomas Morris. It's called "Mormon Battalion Song." This is the old gentleman who went with the battalion and whose diary I commented about. How very exciting!

Oct 21, 1961. I generally take my lunch to our twelve o'clock research class and eat a little when I can — causing everyone great envy. I was sitting by Dave Jacobs yesterday, as is my custom — when for some reason I turned around for a moment, and Dave took my eight-inch ballpoint pen and stabbed it right into my sandwiches (on the table in a plastic bag). When I turned back and saw my pen stuck into my lunch like an arrow shot from an Indian's bow, or a flag fast in the virgin soil of Columbus' New World, I went into hysterics. I couldn't breathe — I couldn't move — I just put my head on the table and laughed uncontrollably.

Dr. Morley stopped his lecture: "Did I say something to amuse you, Miss Wright?"

When I regained control sufficiently to move, I picked up the offended article and gasped: "Dave — stabbed — my sandwiches!"

It was some time before we resumed class.

Oct 31, 1961. I have an idea for my play! The circumstances would be Orderville in the 1870s under the United Order. Possibly it could reflect the human Mormon, basically good but still bearing the flaws of a worldly existence.

Here we see the conception of Carol Lynn's musical, The Order Is Love, *which in the years since its premiere has been produced widely throughout the Church.*

Nov 16, 1961. Yesterday I forgot to mention the Devotional speech. Some of it I enjoyed; but I find I feel rather alien to intense fireballs who serve an audience a neat formula for spirituality and success, tied with obviously sincere clichés, and sporting a neon label: "Exaltation or Bust!"

Nov 21, 1961. I've had another poem accepted for publication! Today I received a letter from the National Poetry Association in Los Angeles saying that they had selected "Exorcism" to be published in the *Annual Anthology of College Poetry.* I'm very glad.

Nov 28, 1961. I rather hope that my mother keeps track of me now and again. There are still many things in me that she would be ashamed of; but I think there are a few more that she might be proud of.

We have talked in several places so far about why people want to keep diaries. Here's yet another reason to think about: Notice that Carol Lynn longs to have her mother know how she's doing. She wants to share her life – her successes in particular, but, more generally, just the fact of her being alive and unique – with someone who cares. Such an impulse is pretty much a universal one. It comes out in strange ways, sometimes: people write their names on fences and walls, if they have no other outlet. Perhaps you have heard the story about the small orphan girl who regularly threw over the orphanage wall notes that read: "Whoever Finds This: I love you." She was asserting her selfhood, as well as her loneliness.

In many cases, a journal serves as an ideal outlet for sharing our lives. We are free to put down what we consider important; we can tell our side of the story, show things from our perspective. Without fear of interruption or contradiction, we can express ourselves as we wish, getting down in black and white feelings that ofttimes we're not ready to share with anyone else yet but still want to "get off our chests."

Very recently I talked with a young career woman who leads a busy, full, and far from lonely life. She said, "My journal has been a really good companion this last year." In other words, a journal can satisfy the need for one very important kind of human dialogue.

Dec 3, 1961. I don't know what our Ninth Ward will do when old Brother Vance dies. He manages to stir things up now and again. This morning at testimony meeting, he arose with, "Harken, oh ye people of Israel," and went on to call the ward to repentance.

Dec 10, 1961. Strange things have been happening today: there is a distinct possibility that I might have a chance to go to New York for the holidays.

Dec 13, 1961. I think I am going! [*To New York.*] I called Fred on the telephone an hour and a half ago; he had received my letter and was very excited about the whole thing. "Come, come — please come," he said. And I feel very good about the whole thing.

Dec 19, 1961. (New York City). What a very full day in New York! Fred and I started the day off beautifully and perfectly, as if it had been written for us. We walked around Central Park and watched the darkness leave the city. The only people there were the statue of Daniel Webster and a few squirrels.

After lunch, we walked down Fifth Avenue and ordered some stationery at Tiffany's for Tammy Grimes. Then I spent the afternoon in the Museum of Modern Art; it was most interesting. Art pieces of every kind, paintings, wood carvings, metal, plastic, photographs, vases, chairs, dishes — and even a moving light display. One thing I got a real kick out of was a huge picture called "Mona Lisa, Age Twelve." The girl portrayed had a huge chubby face, a little abstract body, Mona Lisa eyes, and a tiny mouth drawn up in a weird little smile.

All along the sidewalks are Salvation Army bands, and anemic-looking Santa Clauses ringing bells for contributions. And people dash about insanely. On the bus coming home, I gave my seat to a little old lady, and she nearly fainted.

And then I got on the wrong bus — during the rush hour! The driver gave me a transfer and told me where to catch the bus I wanted. "See that awning over there, where that bunch of people is waiting? Well, you run, get in the middle of them, and kick hard in all directions. And the more people you kill, the bigger success you are." Then he sighed, "I get to retire in twenty-six years."

Dec 22, 1961. I think that Tammy Grimes is a fantastic comedienne! The show itself is cute [*The Unsinkable Molly Brown*], but it would be nothing without her. I don't know when I've seen a play in which a character-ization was so thoroughly digested and assimilated as hers was with Molly Brown.

Dec 24, 1961. President Henry D. Moyle is visiting here and spoke in Church. Fred and I spent the afternoon watching TV and visiting in his apartment. After evening sacrament meeting, we went over to the home of Bob and Lola Redford. We both knew her from Provo, and Bob is currently starring in *Sunday in New York,* a Broadway comedy. Mary Clark and her husband were also there. The Redfords are most in-teresting people, and we talked about many things (acting, school, etc.)

Well, not all of us will be able to thumb through our old journals and find a casual mention of someone quite so famous as Robert Redford. But you never know! And "I-Knew-Them-When" is a lot of fun – especially if you have your diaries as "Exhibit A" in case no one believes you!

Jan 3, 1962. Home — and I'm almost too tired to sleep, so I shall write for a few minutes.

Tom sent me a special dog tag that he had made for me in Korea: "I

79

Am Carol Lynn Wright. Please Drop Me in Nearest Mailbox." I thought this was so funny I stayed awake chuckling.

Jan 7, 1962. This evening our Fine Arts Fireside Group met at Diana Markham's parents' home, and our speaker was Dr. Truman Madsen. It was a most stimulating and profitable experience. He is very encouraging about the place of art in the Church and said that . . . if we keep truly in harmony with the Church and also work diligently on our art, we will be ready to give whenever the time comes that our contribution is needed. Communicating the gospel through the arts will become of prime importance.

Jan 10, 1962. I think I must be the luckiest girl in the world! Exactly five weeks from tonight will be the opening night of *The Lark,* in which I will play Joan of Arc.

Jan 13, 1962. It's not like me to want to give up sleep for anything, but I wish I could stay up for hours to study Joan. I wonder just how much of the legend is true? Did she really act under actual and literal command from heaven? Why not? The idea appeals to me — especially because she was of the race of Woman, whose primary function historically is to go unnoticed.

Jan 15, 1962. As I was scanning the *Daily Universe* today, I came across an article saying that the *Wye Magazine* will be out very soon with the winning poetry and prose selections. I went on to read: "Carol Lynn Wright, a graduate student from Provo and a national prize recipient, is the winner of the poetry division with a compilation of original works."

I must remember to tell my grandchildren about the trials of Woman in 1962, should she attempt to sleep with the present-day hair curlers rolled up in her hair like tiny, ancient Indian spike-beds.

Jan 24, 1962. What fun to start a brand-new diary!

Elder Alma Sonne spoke at Devotional this morning. "Let your light so shine. . . ." But that slogan is almost a little deceptive. A person consists of many, many light globes; how does one know just which ones to turn off and which ones to let shine? This is not a question of good and evil, but of more subtle shades of values. Maybe I burn daily several thousand watts that are sheer waste.

Jan 25, 1962. My word! I've never been through such a rigorous rehearsal as tonight's was! We went over and over the building scene

80

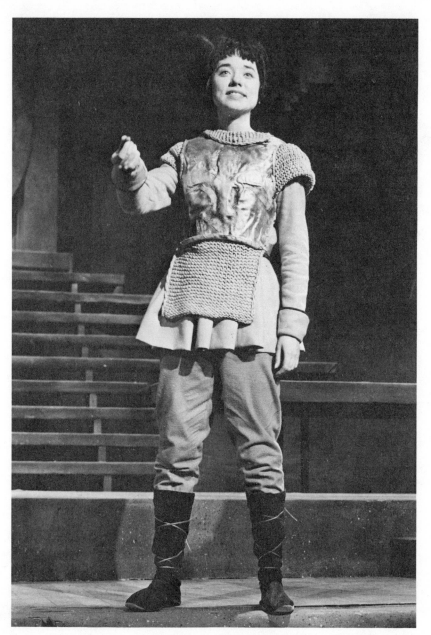

As Joan of Arc in **The Lark**

just before LaHire comes in. I have to be frightened, desperate, help-less — building, building until I break. Dr. Hansen pounded us — pounded us; he got inches away from me and pulled — pulled — until I was drained dry.

Jan 27, 1962. Rehearsal went well this morning — so well, in fact, that I've got bruises all over my arms.

Feb 3, 1962. This afternoon I rewrote my last poem. I like it much better. Perhaps later I'll want to change it, but for now, I'm satisfied.

Joan of Arc

Her fingers were not meant for chafing wrists
Where skin is raw from rusty shackles' bite;
Nor were her lungs intended for the mists
Of filthy dungeons, fouled with tallow light.
Those fingers loved the touch of horse and leaves,
A white sword flashing with her soldier pride;
Those lungs were meant to swell with scent of sheaves
Fresh-harvested in her French countryside.

And though the judgment strained with wisdom's wit
To bow her with the rod of holy birch,
Her soul was not intended to be lit
A sacrificial candle to the Church —
And on the sacred stand her body stole
The flame and died a martyr to her soul.

Feb 14, 1962. In just a few minutes I will go up to prepare for opening night. And just as I was reading my mail, a telegram arrived from Fred. How very, very exciting. Fred is sweet.
"MY THOUGHTS AND PRAYERS WILL BE WITH YOU TONIGHT.

LOVE, FRED"

Here goes!
(Later) It was wonderful. I do feel quite good about it. I received some very good comments afterwards. Dr. Bingham said that it was one of the best pieces of acting he's seen in twenty years.

Feb 15, 1962. I wish our performance would last for months and months. I love it. And I do almost nothing all day long except wait — wait for the overture and the curtain. . . . During my big scene (submis-sion) I cried more than last night. Just before I sink to the floor on "I

82

submit," a great huge tear slid down my cheek and plopped onto the painted canvas and glittered there until it dried at the end of the play.

Feb 21, 1962. Received a letter from Fred today. He said that he's planning on coming home for a while sometime in March or April — and that he's looking for a new and maybe permanent job in New York.

It seems to me now that thoughts of Fred have been in my mind for fifty years. And my mind is now heavy and old and sick — and very, very tired.

Feb 25, 1962. It's snowing outside now — and as I look from my window, I feel almost as if I'm reuniting with an old and dear friend.

Mar 26, 1962. Today was marvelous! I received a letter from Fred that I had no idea he had it in him to write. He gave me a thorough bawling-out for my last letter. A few excerpts for posterity:

"Dear Miss Wright:

"I am in receipt of your last rather cold, classical, and correct epistle, and all I can say is I don't really know what on earth you are talking about. . . .

"You know you have such a great gift for writing, and I love to get your letters because they are always so interesting and newsy and mostly because they give me new insights into you, but at times (and this last letter is a prime example) you have a tendency to be very sarcastic, brittle, and Dorothy Parker-ish — I don't know if you really intend to sound that way or if it just slips out. . . ."

Mar 30, 1962. Today was Fred day. He arrived early. We went to *The Boyfriend* this evening and then talked at my house until after two o'clock. Things are fine. We talked about many important things: in a general way rather than a specific way (I mean as pertains to us).

Apr 21, 1962. Sometimes I say to myself, "You fool. Isn't it obvious that you and Fred do not belong together?" And I usually answer, "Yes, but right now I need him." So then I sneer at myself and say, "Then you're just a selfish coward who is desperately afraid of being alone."

But this isn't always the dialogue that comes. Sometimes I say, "Fred and I do share something that is very good. And it's quite as much my fault as his that we drift along playing blind man's bluff with each other."

It's so hard to go on this way — so hard!

83

May 6, 1962. Today Fred and I ate dinner with Gary and Diana. It was quite nice — but Fred and I are still speaking through cellophane.

May 7, 1962. I want so very much to do that thing which God would most approve of. Where can *I* best contribute? I have prayed about this most earnestly, and I vow that I will do anything that I feel prompted to do. I will go on a mission with no qualms, if I feel God would have me do that. Or I will go into teaching, or I will forget my independent goals and get married.

May 9, 1962.

Haiku

If only snowflakes
Smelled like white lilacs drifting,
Birds would not fly south.

May 13, 1962. Our fine arts fireside group met tonight to hear Crawford Gates. His most significant comment: "Art will always be a matter secondary to the salvation of human souls." And I am closer to this conclusion personally than I have ever been.

May 17, 1962. Tonight I went to the English Awards Banquet to be recognized for my *Wye Magazine* prize. But as it turned out, I also got another award — second honorable mention in the Hart-Larson Poetry Contest.

Dr. P. A. Christensen gave a speech on life and literature. He mentioned the myth of Hercules holding Anteus up away from the earth, because Anteus needed contact with the earth for strength. Literature is Anteus and life is the earth. Separation of the two brings death. What a rare man he is! Although his age shows through somewhat, he is still a most impressive man, with his white crewcut and salty wisdom.

May 19, 1962. This evening was our Speech and Drama Awards Banquet; and for the second year, I won the "Best Actress" award. Brother Clinger presented it, and introduced me as "the First Lady of BYU theater." So I have a beautiful trophy . . . but the beautiful memory won't be of my friends applauding as I received the award; it will be the throbbing of my soul as I created Joan on the stage of the J. S. auditorium — the building of the music as I first entered — and the sliding of a tear onto the painted canvas.

May 22, 1962. My evening with Fred turned out to be quite profitable. We aren't really such strangers as I sometimes think we are. We agree that very soon must come the decision of what is going to happen to us. The things that hold us away from each other are so undefinable that it's hard to analyze the situation. Fred means so much to me. And in some ways, we're so very, very good.

May 27, 1962. Later this evening I read the history that Mother wrote up in the hospital and that Daddy finished for her. It's so sketchy — but some things are very precious — like the three little letters she wrote to us the Christmas before she died. Death is a thing of almost total mystery. But I believe that even now I am not lost to her awareness. And even now she loves me; she has to; she gave me birth.

No more poignant reason can be given for keeping journals than the yearnings of young people whose parents died early. There is a driving need to know our roots, our parents, who they are, and hence who we are. One woman I know lost her father before she was two. He left no journal, no writings. All she has are one or two books he owned, with brief notes pencilled in the margins. She cherishes these books and the notes as her only direct knowledge of her father. Think how joyful she would be to have a journal of his, even if it were only of one year of his life!

May 31, 1962. I attended another shower for Linda tonight. I enjoyed seeing the old group again. And I get along with them much better now than in high school. I have sort of proved myself since high school. Actually, the group of girls that I went through high school with are outstanding. And I could have appreciated them much more if I had not always been so much on the defensive.

Jun 5, 1962. I had a brilliant idea today about my thesis, and Dr. Hansen approved it. Instead of two more one-acts, I shall write a one-hour children's play based on my *Pegora's Plight* assembly. I think it could make a very good children's theater play.

Watch how **Pegora** *takes off from this moment, and how she continues to bring good fortune to her creator.*

Jun 11, 1962. Fred and I are enigmatic absolutely! We are enmeshed in gossamer threads — some that bind us so close we can't separate — some that cover our eyes so we can't see clearly — and some that are across our lips so we're afraid to speak.

Jun 13, 1962. This afternoon I gave a program up at the Relief Society meeting of the State Hospital. I gave very light, simple things, and they seemed to enjoy it. It was held out on the lawn, and I nearly wore out my voice with trying to project and be vivacious.

Jun 14, 1962. No news from the Kalamazoo Civic Theater. I was sort of expecting that I might receive an assistantship. HMMMM. *Nothing* that I plan for next year seems to happen. Is my guardian angel saving me for something better? Or am I just a twenty-two-year-old failure?

Jun 17, 1962. Once in a while I experience a new dawn of enlightenment that makes me think that a great deal of what has been wrong with Fred and me is my own fault. I really can't make this at all specific, but I *know* that it's true.

One thing Fred said last night made me think a little. I live in extremes, he said — either very giddy or else terribly serious. I think that's probably true. And it's not good.

Jun 25, 1962. This evening I gave a program for the MIA at the State Hospital: "How Br'er Rabbit Lost His Long, Bushy Tail," "The Waltz," and "Laffing." They seemed to enjoy them very much. Afterwards I stayed and danced with them for a while.

Jul 3, 1962. My orals went fine. My four interrogators touched on only a tiny fraction of all that I've been studying so diligently. It got a bit deep for me only when Dr. Larson began asking me about who was responsible for justifying art to the church at the end of the middle ages. For some reason — and I'll never understand it — the name of St. Thomas Aquinas came to my mind — and that's who he wanted. I know *nothing* about the man — and why I thought of him, I'll never know. Miscellania they asked me: romanticism, naturalism, eighteenth-century actors, threshing-floor theory, epic theater, acting of poetic drama, modern directors, modern designers, etc.

Jul 8, 1962. It's a vicious circle: one cannot feel close to God when one is wretched, and not feeling close to God makes one wretched.

Jul 17, 1962. I have now typed twenty-two pages of my thesis. This is what has occupied most of my time as of late. It certainly is a nerve-wracking experience — eight copies, seven carbons: make a mistake and you're dead! Last night I stayed up until 1 A.M. typing.

Jul 24, 1962 (Ephraim, Utah). I am writing this from Banana and

Duane's house in Ephraim. I am here for the next week and a half to play Opal in Duane's play, *Everybody Loves Opal,* by John Patrick.

Yesterday I finished typing my thesis and took it up to Dr. Larson to sign.

Jul 27, 1962. Our rehearsal for *Opal* is coming pretty well. I spent a couple of hours on lines yesterday morning and went without my book in the afternoon in the first two acts. Now I've got all my lines down — some of them a little shaky, but I'm rid of my book. This part looks so huge that just for sport I counted my speeches — there are 314 speeches, some of them quite long — she's a very verbose character. I'm so glad I don't have any trouble memorizing.

Aug 1, 1962. Tonight was our first performance of *Everybody Loves Opal,* and — everybody loved Opal. I enjoy my characterization of Opal — it's terrific fun to play an eccentric with a heart of gold who lives in a junkyard.

Aug 9, 1962. Fred and I have just parted. We have agreed not to see each other again — at least not in the definable future. We sat over on the school lawn and talked. And although this seems to be the only decision we could reach, my heart is sobbing within me — and I know his is, too, this moment as he is walking home. We love each other dearly; we will pray for each other always, and we want each other to be happy always — so very happy.

Aug 10, 1962. Duane is coming for me tomorrow, and he and Banana and I are leaving from Ephraim for L. A. on Monday. I don't want to take this diary with me. It is too full of Fred. I want to buy a new empty diary for my new empty life and make them full — both my diary and my life.

7

"My pen will help me get perspective"

Music was to change radically in the 1960s, but for the week of September 6, 1962, the best-selling records still indicated fairly traditional trends: Johnny Mathis, Johnny Cash, Jimmy Dean, the Everly Brothers – and a new voice that would become important: Chubby Checker. Also high on the popularity charts was an album by the Mormon Tabernacle Choir, featuring their splendid version of "The Battle Hymn of the Republic." Carol Lynn's own interest in music picked up this year: she began taking singing lessons! Though all of her own acting roles had been in straight comedy and drama, the plays she would write a few years hence would be predominantly musicals: The Order Is Love, I Was a P.O.W. in the Battle of the Sexes, My Turn on Earth, *and so forth.*

Aug 18, 1962.

Haiku

I would sleep but thoughts
Cling to my mind like beetles
That will not shake loose.

Sep 6, 1962. Well, I have now committed the next nine months of my life to Snow College, Ephraim, Utah. Director Holme and I finally agreed on a salary of $4,800.

And now, before I forget, I must record a little item about Tom that his old roommate told me. It seems that Tom was having financial struggles in school about two years ago. So he took his winter jacket down to Deseret Industries and told the lady he wanted to sell it.

Lady: But you don't understand. We don't buy things. People give us things and then we distribute them to those who are less well off.

Tom: Oh. Well, here.

He handed her the jacket and walked out. Dear Tom! My very, very dear Tom. I hope he finds something wonderful in life.

Sep 7, 1962.

Haiku

Old apple tree nods
In the breeze, drugged by the scent
Of its own blossoms.

Sep 10, 1962. So now I am a college instructor. I walked down to the post office to mail a card to Daddy earlier, and for the first time I tried to look at the town of Ephraim as if it belonged to me. I even introduced myself to the postmaster, said hello to a small boy on a bicycle, and smiled at several strange people.

Sep 12, 1962. Here I sit in the new apartment of Bob and Dorothy Hicks. They went to a movie tonight in celebration of their fourth anniversary, so I agreed to tend their children. I brought along this book because this may be the last night I'll have a chance to write without the immediate pressure of getting my classes ready, and I did want to take a deep breath and let my pen help me get perspective before I forge ahead.

We have seen Carol Lynn use her diaries to gain insight on the past; here she is using them as a way of sizing up the future and making long-range goals.

Sep 25, 1962. Tonight I gave my *Medea* to the adult class of the West Ward MIA. I think it went over very well. I never cease to marvel at the adjectives chairwomen can find for *Medea*. [Medea *is a violent tragedy in which, among other things, the title character kills her children to spite her husband.*] Tonight's chairwoman said, "Thank you so much; it was just — just — charming!"

Sep 27, 1962. My birthday. What special things have I done since I became twenty-two?

—Well, I started and finished requirements for a Master's Degree in Dramatic Arts, finishing my college career with a cumulative grade-point average of 3.89.

89

—I wrote two plays.

—I spent a magnificent two-week Christmas holiday in New York with my dear Fred.

—I created the most successful role that I have ever done, Joan in *The Lark,* and had some interesting experiences with Opal and Medea.

—I wrote a few good poems, and had one translated into French and published in Paris.

—I went through the vicissitudes of friendship — seeing Selene go off, watching Joan elope to the temple, suffering through Mary Anne's pregnancy, and shipping Tom off to Korea.

—My family is still intact, with all of the boys still attending the Y and Marie working in Salt Lake City.

—And I lost Fred. But not before we had some beautiful times together, and some very unhappy times as well.

—Quite suddenly, too, I became a college instructor and have made my home — for a year — in Ephraim.

Dear Twenty-Four:

I give you a year. If it is not happy and productive when you finish with it, it's nobody's fault but your own. You have too much just to fail by chance.

Devotedly,
Twenty-Three.

Oct 1, 1962. Today I received my first paycheck for an honest-to-goodness job — $360.68. Exactly one-fourth of my salary is gone before I even see the check. Still, I intend to save $2,500 of this year's salary for Europe.

Oct 15, 1962. I'm pleased with an assignment I made to my freshman English classes: keeping somewhat of a diary with daily entries on some observation they'd made. Only a few students disappointed me; and many surprised me with more than I'd expected. I wish I could persuade them to keep a real, true journal.

No better endorsement can be made for journal-keeping than this one from Carol Lynn, who had at this point been keeping a record for over six years.

Another idea worth noting: she writes, "Many surprised me with more than I'd expected." If you are one who says, "I wouldn't be any good at keeping a journal," take her words to heart. You'll surprise yourself with more than you'd expected.

90

Oct 26, 1962. I wanted to record a comment from Shaw's *Major Barbara* that gave me a slight jolt of truth: "You have learned something, and that always feels at first as if you have lost something."

Oct 27, 1962. This afternoon, Banana and I went bicycle riding. The weather was no less than magnificent, and we rode along the country roads admiring horses, haystacks, and turkeys.

Oct 29, 1962. On the way home [*back from Provo*], I killed an elk with Duane's car. Eight miles north of Fairview, there suddenly loomed three huge animals on the road in front of us. I slammed on the brakes, but hit one with the right fender. When I finally stopped, we were nearly facing the other way on the highway, and the car wouldn't start, so I got it off the road and down into the barrow pit. In a couple of minutes, a man stopped and tried to help us, then drove us into Fairview. I told my students about it this morning and was a sensation.

Oct 30, 1962.

Haiku

Rooster crows until
Dusk — forever astonished
At the creeping sun.

(Truly — I did hear roosters all day long.)

Nov 8, 1962. Yesterday Eleanor Roosevelt died. Adlai Stevenson: "She would rather light candles than curse the darkness."

Nov 21, 1962. I drove to Provo this afternoon with Mr. Crane, and spent the rest of the day preparing the decorations for Marie's wedding. I went up to Helen's for a while and talked with her about the plans. Aunt Mamie and Uncle Wesley were there.

Nov 28, 1962. One of the books my class is reading is *The Diary of Anne Frank*. I think this book is a magnificent piece of work. And whenever I read it, I feel a sense of shame for my own insignificant book. Anne had a right to record herself. She was a significant soul writing from a significant situation. And I fear this is not my case. Except of course, that I am a living person existing on God's earth; this, in and of itself, has staggering implications. So I suppose I shall continue these exercises.

Do you remember Emily, in Thornton Wilder's Our Town? *It is only after her death, when she is allowed to return to life, to one day in her life, that she realizes how beautiful and precious the simplest moments and the simplest actions are. Once we have acquired the habit of recording our lives, we view our lives a little differently. We see a little of what Emily saw, and what Carol Lynn saw: life's "staggering implications."*

Dec 3, 1962. I told my freshmen there were two kinds of clauses today: main clauses and Santa Clauses. Probably some of them believed me.

Dec 20, 1962. (Provo). In the little pile of mail that Daddy handed me Sunday was a letter from Fred. He will be home for the holidays (in fact, is here now), and wants to come and see me.

Dec 22, 1962. I am looking at the old nativity set that is in its traditional place on our television. Each piece looks so sad that I fear it might be time to dispose of them. Too many gluings have put each shepherd's chin down into his cloak. The brown cow's ears are nothing but little white pits. Mary's nose is scratched, and Joseph's forehead. The angel looks as if it got caught in an olive tree on its way down. The wise men from the East look poverty-stricken, and their camels seem to have contracted some rare disease. The little stable still is quite sturdy, however, and the Baby Jesus is still perfectly intact. So perhaps the discarding time has not yet arrived.

Dec 23, 1962. The other day I saw in the newspaper the wedding announcement of one of my students, and I thought, *How on earth can he get married?* He's practically illiterate and doesn't deserve the D I gave him.

But it happens all the time. The odds are even for it happening to me. Again — this is beyond my grasp.

Dec 26, 1962.

Renewal

I think each night my body sleeps
My soul flies up to God,
Whose touch instills sufficient faith
To meet the day ahead.

This idea also shows up in a later poem, "Lullabye of the Heavenly Mother."

92

Dec 27, 1962. Fred called this afternoon and asked to see me tonight. I had to give a program for a group in Spanish Fork, so he came with me. I gave a Christmas program, and it went over very well. I did not know what to expect of Fred; everything was just as it had been at our very, very *best* moments. We sat in my house and talked about everything until 1:15 — school, teaching, a thousand related subjects, things we'd done, people we know, states of being. I told him essentially all I had considered about us — how both of us had done far too much waiting and far too little building, etc. Basically, he agreed.

I'm so glad we saw each other tonight — so glad. The thing sets a little easier in my soul.

Jan 12, 1963. At about 6:30 I received a long-distance phone call.
Me: Hello?
Voice: Miss Carol Lynn Wright?
Me: Yes.
Voice: Go ahead, please.
Other Voice: This is a Salt Lake operator. I have a telegram here from Ogden signed "Jazbo." It reads: "Good luck tonight, Magnolia. I'll see you next weekend, weather permitting."

How pleasant that fate chooses excellent moments to let Larry pop back into my life. I know he'll pop right back out again, but it *is* pleasant.

Jan 27, 1963. Yesterday I had a conference with Mr. Golightly about *Pegora*. As Mr. G. and I were talking, in came Chuck Henson with his sketches for the set; they looked very good. It was really quite exciting to sit there while a director and a scene designer talked production for *my* play! I felt like something out of *Act One*.

The mail today brought a letter from Fred. It was, of course, very good to hear from him. It's not easy to go on living and loving with heart open but hands closed.

Jan 31, 1963. (Ephraim). Last night I taught my first class in creative writing. And I think I can say it went very well.

Now it is past midnight, but I must write, else I shall become a sloth. I just returned from Moroni, where Nathalie Hansen and I gave a program on Korea and Japan. Often at these clubs, I sit and think how I would like to capture some of this dialogue for a play:

"Poor Caroline — all that's happened to her in the last six years is an appendicitis, two miscarriages, and four kids."

93

Talking about nursing homes: "Boy, you'll never get me into one of those. They cut everybody's hair just alike, and all they feed you is Jell-O."

Feb 4, 1963. I received material today from the London Academy of Music and Dramatic Arts (LAMDA). How I wish things might work out for me to attend this or one of the other academies in London!

Feb 7, 1963. Janet told me today that one of the boys in her English class that I've been conducting says I talk like a foreigner and it bothers him.

Feb 16, 1963. (Provo). I think it is justifiable to spend a dollar a week for a hair shampoo and set — if only for the time it saves during the week.

How very exciting to watch rehearsals for a play one has written! I spent the entire afternoon at College Hall watching *Pegora* rehearsals.

Feb 23, 1963. I like to spend Saturday mornings with my mind closed, singing while doing little physical things.

Feb 27, 1963. Tonight saw me whizzing toward Provo in an ambulance to see the premiere performance of *Pegora*. I was in an ambulance only because I rode up with Marge Hafen, who runs Mayfield Manor in Mayfield. I took my creative writing class up. Mrs. Hafen presented me with a corsage of carnations and roses. I sat at the back, chewing Dave Jacobs' fingernails, cursing the light men and the music coordination, and dying when the show seemed to drag. But it was all very exciting to observe the opening of a play that sprang from my very own mind.

Mar 1, 1963. *Pegora* was much better tonight than it was Wednesday. And there I was, with my new green suit on, and corsage, and *autographing programs!*

Mar 2, 1963. I wonder if there might be more future for me in writing than in any other phase of the theater!

Mar 17, 1963. I failed six of my freshman English students. I could not find an excuse in the world to pass any of them.

Mar 18, 1963. This morning in the library, I looked up Alan Napier in *Who's Who in the Theater.* This is the gentleman who will hear me audition for LAMDA on March 30. I finally determined which two scenes I will give: Rosalind from *As You Like It* for the Shakespeare, and Joan from *Saint Joan* for the modern.

Mar 31, 1963. (Beverly Hills, California). I was at the Stage Society

Theater this morning when Mr. Napier arrived, and as someone else was using the hall, we sat for a while in the anteroom and talked. Mr. Napier is a very tall man with gray hair and a beautiful English voice, a distinguished bearing, and a pleasant manner.

I had been absolutely petrified all day — so nervous I could hardly eat — and living in continuous prayer. But always, when my feet are actually on the boards of a stage, fear dissolves, and some indefinable opposite takes over. I took thirty seconds to compose myself and began to play Rosalind quite as gaily and vivaciously as I could. The three minutes were over in a second, and the scene was finished.

I also did a scene from *Saint Joan* and one from *Glass Menagerie.* After I had finished, Mr. Napier told me again how very stiff the competition is and that only four places in the advanced course are for girls, and that two of those have already been taken by the Fulbright winners.

"All I can do is send my report and tell them that you obviously have great talent. The final decision is theirs."

Again I ponder the difference between dictating to God and demonstrating the kind of faith that works miracles. And I think I must believe this way: I have no right to assert complete faith that God will give me this blessing. But I do have a right to assert complete confidence that this decision will not be left to chance or human impulse. I have the right to know that in something this momentous, God's judgment, and none else's, will rule. This I can know, and really, this is all I need.

Apr 12, 1963. I received a letter from LAMDA, with regrets that they cannot offer me a place in the course. I am so entirely confused.

Apr 17, 1963. I've developed a terribly materialistic habit: opening new savings accounts at places that give free gifts. Today I sent a $200 check to Deseret Federal in Salt Lake, from whom I will receive a G. E. heating pad. I'm sure it shows something highly revealing about my character that I should choose a heating pad over a crystal salad set or bathroom scales.

Some time ago, I received an ovenwear set from First Federal (with whom I now have $300) and a set of steak knives from Utah Savings and Loan in Provo (with whom I have $500). So I now have $1,000 besides the nearly $1,300 that is frozen in Guaranty.

Apr 26, 1963. I received a note from Dave Jacobs today plus a $15 check

95

for writing the BYU Fine Arts Assembly — *Fruition*, a parable about plants and talents. Let's see — this makes my writing income add up to:

$ 4 Fourth-grade essay on "Eating a Good Breakfast"
$10 First Prize — BYU Poetry Contest
$30 BYU Royalty for *Pegora*
$15 BYU assembly — *Fruition*

Rather an unimpressive list, but at least it's a beginning.

May 5, 1963. Most of the time that my mind is otherwise unoccupied I spend contemplating the future. How I wish I could receive a special delivery letter from God saying what I should do. I have thought very seriously about staying on in Europe after the tour — traveling around, writing, or studying somewhere until my funds run out. But today, as at other times, I've been contemplating going on a mission. Truly I want to do that thing which is *most* worthwhile.

Here is another instance of tiny seeds which sprout up years later. Those of you who know CLWP's musical, My Turn on Earth, *will recognize the "special delivery letter from God" as one of the delightful pieces of business therein.*

May 13, 1963. I told the director today that I am not planning on coming back next year. He seemed disappointed but quite understanding about my reasons. I told him I simply want to do something adventurous before the possibility is gone.

May 31, 1963. This year has been good for me because it demanded that I meet a whole new situation and construct a whole new world. This I have done, and I have become quite fond of that world: Mr. Jennings, Miss Phillips, Fonda Stout in the bookstore, Doris in the office, and, of course, Janet and Mr. and Mrs. C. [*the family with whom CLW lived*]. I will even miss my office with the white leather couch, my big double bed with the flowered bedspread, the train that whistles at midnight, the grain factory I passed by every day on my way to school, and the sheep, cows, and horses here and there that I like to say hello to.

Jun 6, 1963. And now my brother Warren is married; very strange to think about.

Jun 8, 1963. I am sitting with my feet in the oven of my new temporary home [*in Cedar City*] studying my lines for Rosalind. There are nearly fifty participants here [*in the annual Shakespearean Festival*], and I've met many that I know I will like. I adore my part; Rosalind is a wonderful, wonderful role. [*Rosalind is the heroine of Shakespeare's* As You Like It.]

Jun 11, 1963.

Lament

To security's search
There is no answer:
Mosquitoes get slapped
And the Pope gets cancer.

Jun 23, 1963. I attended stake conference this morning and heard Elder Spencer W. Kimball lecture vehemently on buying flags, not letting young girls go to Salt Lake to work, and sending every young boy into the mission field.

Jul 8, 1963. O Jupiter, how weary is my body and how exhilarated is my spirit! What a frustration not to be able to verbalize how intensely I adore acting! Acting, being in love, and searching out God are the only mountains in the plain of my existence. Tonight I frolicked atop the mountain of acting, and found myself so high up that I was giddy with the thin air and trembling with the nearness of the clouds.

Jul 9, 1963. I sold horehound, oranges, and tarts tonight [*at the Shakespearean Festival*], and made quite a production of it . . . fell into me Cockney and gave them "a bit of a show." And I sold more than anyone else did.

Jul 10, 1963. Well, I made the *Deseret News* for my performance as a horehound seller. Mr. Chaffin wrote that the audience was greatly amused at Rosalind of the night before (Carol Lynn Wright) selling with a very authentic Cockney accent.

Jul 20, 1963. I have sold me last tarts, oranges, and horehound. A few days ago a lady called me over —

Lady: I've just got to ask you — is that accent real?
Me: Only me 'airdresser knows for sure!

Jul 25, 1963. (Provo). How excited I am! I did more sewing today, went to see Dr. Aaron, did a few sundry things — and the day is gone. I have one more day at home, and a thousand things to do. My mind is in a panic!

Jul 26, 1963. In a couple of minutes, Dave will be by for me, and I'M OFF FOR EUROPE!

8

"A new book, a new era"

By the summer of 1963, the volatile decade of change was well launched. Some changes were good: American blacks, for instance, were getting an improved quality of education. And things were about to change for young women. For example: a small news item from the week of July 29, 1963, when Carol Lynn was beginning her big European adventure, reported that at a United States-USSR track and field meet, while American men did fairly well, American women failed to get a single first-place medal. But within a few years, girls and women in the United States would be starting to get the support and training that would bring them to the forefront in international sports.

Other changes of the sixties, however, were tragic ones. While in Russia, for example, Carol Lynn would learn of the assassination of President John F. Kennedy – the beginning of a storm of violence that would last throughout the decade and that would taint the entire world. When I asked Carol Lynn, as we were putting this book together, if she would feel comfortable today about having a daughter of hers make the trip Carol Lynn herself made in 1963 – on her own in Europe and the Mideast for a year – she said, emphatically, "Of course not!"

Jul 29, 1963 (New York City). How I miss my real true big green diary! This notebook feels fake, but I must make it do. Here we are in bed — four of us in a room at the YWCA. Our bus trip was blah, as are most trips by bus.

Jul 30, 1963. What a wonderful evening I have just spent! Fred and I had a marvelous time going to a play and then chasing around afterward. On a bench down in Greenwich Village, we had quite a good talk. I told him about my plans and he told me about his. Everything has been very good between us these three days, just as I knew they would be. And I'm so glad. We're remarkable — he and I — remarkable.

Aug 1, 1963. Plane motors are drumming beneath my feet, and my ears are popping. It's frightening to have nothing between you and solid earth but the hand of God. Frightening and comforting.

Aug 11, 1963. Almost every time I try to use my French, the people reply to me in English, so it's quite discouraging. Once I asked a lady a question, and she said to me (in English): "I don't speak Italian." Great!

Quatrain

> Over
> The continents
> Like a loose ball of yarn
> The past unwinds and slides from my
> Pocket.

Aug 15, 1963. What a complete sin to have fog high in the Swiss Alps! We arrived here at Stanserhorn last night about eight, after a breathtaking train trip up the face of the mountain. As we rode up, it seemed to me we could see half the world — the beautiful half: gorgeous mountain peaks, pine trees, wildflowers, and, as we got to the top, the lake below us and the lights of Lucerne.

> In Europe With a 26-Member Tour
>
> my weight is at least three ton
>
> nine hands and fifteen feet
> do clumsy things
> my mind did not commission
>
> a dozen eyes
> all out of focus
> peer from my head
>
> ears
> (an odd number)
> fly open when I would think
> and close when I would speak

assorted tongues
wag endlessly
occasionally changing rhythm
but never silent
somewhere
hidden in this freakish body
there is a grain
that swells and strains for
heaven

when I can be
only
me
again.

Aug 16, 1963. I think I want to honeymoon in Switzerland. And if my husband can't afford it, I'll sell my silverware.

Aug 22, 1963. Oh, the pain! I have a thousand things to write, and no time to write them in. But there is one thing I must write: I have won first prize in the Utah Fine Arts Institute Creative Writing Contest — children's play division! My *Pegora* — my beautiful, beautiful *Pegora* — has earned me $150! I am thrilled, excited, riddled with joy, and every other cliché.

Aug 25, 1963. The shopping in Florence is an incurable disease. After learning that I had won $150, I went out and spent every cent of it. I have never gone on a giant splurge like this. But I fell in love with an original ceramic figurine — about sixteen inches high — of Arlechino, the mischievous servant of the *commedia del arte*. So with my *Pegora* money, I bought him — for about $40. Unheard of in my existence! But I thought *Pegora* would approve.

Sep 4, 1963. We have just left the most staggeringly beautiful castle imaginable: Ludwig's Castle Linderhof. It's indescribable. Not huge and forbidding like the French or English castles. But while it's before my eyes, I must mention the water we have just seen. Perhaps Thoreau could do it justice — I cannot. Turquoise blue that makes one's heart beat faster — evolving from lakes to rivers as we drive along. This country is gorgeous. What I've seen of Germany so far, I love.

Sep 13, 1963 (Denmark). Early this morning we deposited our things in the hostel and went into town. First we went through the home of

Hans Christian Andersen and the museum. And across the street from the museum was a bakery with the most delicious hot breads.

We have now crossed the water by ferry (seagulls overhead and cold, cold legs) and are approaching Copenhagen. The mountain ash trees along the way are lovely with their bright red berries, the houses are clean and neat, and the cows look happy in the pastures.

Sep 14, 1963. And Tivoli — marvelous! I watched the pantomime show and very much enjoyed it. Nothing is more contrived than this sort of thing, but much of all comedy is based on it. Afterwards, we bought ice cream and walked around the park. I remember:

— The little old lady jumping with the beat of the music outside the dance plaza.

— Two couples in another dance plaza dancing with skill and grace instead of the American sloppiness.

— The gorgeous lanterns of all shapes, sizes, and colors that made the place a wonderland.

— The concert in one of the outdoor areas, playing an American medley. I sat down on the ground in front and waved at the conductor.

Sep 16, 1963 (Stockholm). Dave and I walked around and came across the theater supposed to be the most modern in all Europe. And may I say I was mightily impressed. In progress was Moliere's *Imaginary Invalid,* and we went in to see the last half of it. The theater is truly wonderful — warm brown wood walls, ceiling of the same, red upholstered seats with high backs, not one having any possible obstruction in view. Our blond usher was very nice and told us about the theater. He even opened the side area and showed us how they move the walls to accommodate whatever size audience they wish. Capacity is 1,700. The play was great fun. It was much more animated and ingeniously done than the one in Paris.

Dave and I had a good talk on the boat, about a number of things. He is really a unusual person — a thing of beauty and a joy forever. I think I don't know anybody more thoroughly good and charitable.

Sep 19, 1963. At this moment, the tour group I have been with for two months is in New York City, and I am in an apartment overlooking one of Amsterdam's canals. I said goodbye to them this morning. As I helped them load the luggage on the bus, the driver started away and we all shouted, "Stop! Halt!" So he stopped and halted and I got off and blew my nose and here I am.

101

Sep 21, 1963. Selene's letter suggested that I come from Athens to Nairobi and stay with them. In a way, this sounds great.

This evening I went to the municipal theater to see Frederick Durrenmatt's *The Physicist*. A fellow in line beside me volunteered to sit with me and explain what was going on. So he, his fiancee, and I sat together, and he explained generally what was happening. They were both very kind, and we had an interesting visit. Dutch theater is state-supported, as is the case in many countries. I wish this were so in America.

Sep 25, 1963. I am writing now from a compartment of a train. Here I am with four Greeks with whom I will be until I reach Athens. One of them speaks a little English, but the others none. The major item of interest here is the rather handsome young man sitting across from me who has been trying to communicate all afternoon. But the best we've been able to do is use my phrase book a little, and stand at the window pointing at objects and teaching one another the Greek and English names for them, and making absurd pantomime gestures. What a wretched state of affairs that Tower of Babel brought about!

Sep 26, 1963. How can I possibly describe the frustrating night I have just passed!? And what an idiot I am, for I must take some blame.

The five of us had to sleep here in this compartment, and after several adjustments, this is how we ended up: the young couple on the halves of the benches by the window, the older man on the floor, and Tarro and I opposite one another on the halves of the benches by the door.

Being stretched out in the best way I could (with my feet resting on the old man's stomach), I let my arm drop over the side and in a moment, I felt Tarro's hand right against mine. *How charming*, I thought. *Not able to communicate all day, we can have one moment of pleasant communication without words.* So I didn't move my hand. After a moment, I realized that he was not going to be a passive hand-holder. So I casually withdrew and turned over, as if I'd been asleep all the time. But it was too late.

Before I could breathe again, he was off his bench and kneeling beside me, being immensely affectionate. When I had roused myself from the first shock, I had a huge impulse to laugh riotously. I mean, it was all so ludicrous — here I was in a train compartment, speeding through Germany to Athens, not a soul I knew anywhere, my feet

102

rising and falling with the breathing of a strange man, and a handsome young Greek trying to kiss me.

Immediately, I called to my aid all the verbal negatives I knew: NO! NAY! NIX! NEIN! NYET! accompanying them with pantomime, pushing away, slapping of hands, etc.

But it was clear he didn't take me seriously. And even if I'd known the Greek for one of Elaine Cannon's splendid remarks — such as "I only kiss boys in blue ties," or "Why don't we go bowling instead?" — I don't think it would have been very effective. Yes, I could have screamed, or slammed my fist in his face with all my might, and had he been nasty or crude, I certainly would have. But he was very pleasant and good-natured, and I'm sure he meant no harm. So the only violence I resorted to was a determined tone, stuffing my pillow into his face, and changing my posture, pulling my coat entirely over my head and arms. I've never gone through anything like this in my entire life, and I hope I never shall again. (This new pen I write with now is the possession of the subject of this little essay, who is sitting beside me smoking his one-hundredth cigarette of the day.)

Sep 27, 1963. I dislike immensely writing in red ink, but as I must I shall permit it on the grounds that today is a red-letter day — the twenty-fourth anniversary of my birth. I am noting this event in a rather cluttered train compartment in the country of Greece. Besides innumerable hanging and balancing objects, the compartment is cluttered with me; the Greek man on whose stomach my feet were resting the other night, and who smells at least three days worse than when he got on; and six very young Greek sailors wearing the white uniform and black sash of this tribe.

On this noteworthy anniversary of my birth I find myself in a most peculiar situation: I enter into the city of Athens for what I intend to make a very rich experience. True to my calloused wit in time of crisis, may I say that as I enter I leave behind all things of the world — or, to put it more realistically, I have lost my luggage — or, to be quite exact, my suitcase was stolen. More later. Let us see if I can bear up.

Sep 29, 1963. What a marvelous thing it is that the Church is practically universal and that there is an immediate, automatic bond that unites the membership. People one has never seen before are immediately friends. And help of any kind is spontaneous.

Today we went to the Acropolis. What a perfect thrill to be there in the Theater of Dionysus where so many magnificent things went on!

103

Oct 8, 1963. Yesterday I spent about *four hours* in the office of a Russian travel agency waiting to talk to somebody about the possibility of taking a trip into the USSR. Finally, when I talked to the man through a Greek interpreter, I was told of various tours that interest me mightily: especially a ten-day tour called a "theatrical tour," covering Moscow, Leningrad, Kiev, and back to Moscow. This costs $187 (plus transportation to and from Moscow). This is a huge amount of money, but the idea positively fascinates me.

While waiting, I was first brought a lemonade, then a few hours later an orangeade. And the white-haired man who finally helped me would look at me from behind his desk and smile at me reassuringly with an abrupt, "My darling."

There is no minotaur at my heels, but I am forever in a labyrinth as far as physically getting around in this world goes. I mean, really — *nobody* has such an intense talent for getting lost as I do. It's just something I was blessed with, and since there seems to be no earthly cure I guess I'd better learn to love and cherish it.

Oct 9, 1963. All day long I have been reading Edith Hamilton's *The Greek Way*. It is a marvelous book, and I am now half through. I've gone slowly because I've taken careful notes in one of my little one-drachma tablets. Today I have learned so much that I am invigorated and exhausted.

Oct 15, 1963. As a breeze touches the tree under which I sit, the green needles touch the skyline of Athens. And directly below me is the birthplace of my passionate love — drama. Here on the hillside of the Acropolis I look down on the area where first were heard the voices of Medea, Oedipus, Prometheus, and many other monumental figures. The Theater of Dionysus. I have the marvelous place all to myself — except for a few October tourists that have come for a brief visit.

Today I came to see *Aristophanes*. Of course I had to direct it, costume it, and act it all myself — but it was great fun. Yesterday was *Agamemnon* day. I read it from my shady seat, reading aloud all the lines of Clytemnestra and Cassandra. Just as I was finishing, a young man came over and we had a marvelous two-hour visit. He works as a sound-effects man for the BBC [*British Broadcasting Company*] and has a master's degree in Greek and Roman classics. We went down onto the stage and read a scene from *Agamemnon*. I was Clytemnestra and he was my husband returning from the Trojan War. Then from the top I listened to him do a scene from *Julius Caesar,* and he heard me do a speech from *Medea.* So there I was on ancient holy ground, shouting out to empty, broken-stone seats, evergreen trees, and David Turner. I loved it. We both left thoroughly satisfied with a choice experience. I love to meet new people — when the communication is real.

Oct 21, 1963. I am sitting under a drier in a Greek hairdressing parlor. I have just met the original Ugly American. She soared into the beauty parlor on a jet frown, verbalized in a strange Chicago accent. [*"Ugly American," by way of clarification, was a term used in the sixties for any American traveling or residing in a foreign country who made himself or herself "ugly" by criticizing that country, by loudly announcing America's superiority in everything, and by generally behaving boorishly.*]

"Is there *anybody* here that speaks English? Anybody? I need a wash and set, you understand? My hair is dirty from the boat, very, very dirty. Really, nobody here speaks English. In every other country they all speak English — even the women in the vegetable markets. But here? Nobody! Well, it's gonna cut their tourist trade way down, I can tell you, if somebody in this country doesn't start learning *English.* Well, we're leaving tomorrow — I'm starving to death. I can't eat a thing here, not a thing. It's nothing but oil — nothing but *garbage.*

"We just had a three-day Mediterranean cruise to the islands — and what did we have? Storm — wind — well, just goes to show. And today? The sun. Well — But don't go to the islands. I mean, Mykonos is nothing, *nothing.* A few shops selling those Grecian purses. Well, it's deserted — no people — nothing happening. It's a summer resort, you know. But now it's nothing — nothing! Well, we're getting out tomorrow. And my husband blames *me* for everything. Now this storm could have happened any time, couldn't it?

"Brush — brush very hard. My hair is dirty — very dirty. Do you have a book so I can show you what I want? Good. Well, now I'm sure you won't have anything here I like, but this is the idea." (Hands and fingers and swooping motions. Then she had one of the girls take her to the local restroom, and she returned white, but not speechless.)

"You can't know what I have just been through. Would you believe it — I had to stand up! And there was *no toilet paper.* I'm not a woman used to luxuries. We're a medium family of medium circumstances. And I've never pampered myself. But I must say that I *do* like toilet paper — yes, I do like *toilet paper.*

"My two daughters want to go abroad. But I'm certainly going to tell them a few things. Switzerland was gorgeous. Italy I absolutely adored — but Greece — nothing! What do they have here? Sure, I read about the Acropolis and the temples and, sure, it's nice to see them — but, I mean — no toilet paper!

"Have you been buying things, dear? Maybe you could send something home to your parents. They'd appreciate that, you know."

Well, this went on and on interminably. I'm sure she's a very nice lady and contributes to a charity or two and will be a very generous grandmother, but she just happens to be a Very Ugly American.

Today I paid the deposit on my long-deliberated trip to Russia.

Nov 6, 1963. The shoreline of Mykonos is to my right as I sit at a tiny cafe with my two friends, waiting for our omelet and sausage. There is no sound here but the purr of a motorboat far off, the lapping of the water on the rocks, and the rustle of wind in the tall plants. The people I am with I met last night on the boat: Therese, a Swiss girl who has come here to paint, and Jim Orem, just released from the United States Army. We arrived on the island in a rather remarkable fashion. Some people miss bus stops, but not too many people miss boat stops. Well, we did. We were down below talking, and by the time we got upstairs, the boat was pulling away from the island.

The Man Up There: Mykonos? You want Mykonos? Where is Mykonos? (Pointing to the island we were just leaving.)

At any rate, they put us on a little boat that had come out to get some cargo. Picture of the Day: Me, on a too-small motorboat, cringing as a hook right above us lowered trunk after trunk and pushed us lower and lower into the water. I was one scared CLW. But we made it okay, and it's just one of those marvelous adventures that every traveler ought to have.

Nov 7, 1963. At 5:20 this morning, our landlord, Demetrius, came knocking on the door, and Therese and I hurriedly dressed and followed him down the little white quiet streets to the dock where his two fellow-fishermen were waiting in the boat. As we pulled away from the island, the sight was enchanting: all was dark but for a few lights on the hillside and one beautifully illuminated windmill that got smaller and smaller as we putt-putted away. Then as the sun began to rise, the water turned pink, and the moon paled with the brightening sky. They cast their nets off one of the little islands of Delos, and I watched as they drew them in and put the fish all over the floor of the boat. While they were fishing, they let Therese and me out at one of the islands and we wandered around for a while. It was an uninhabited island, showing still quite a few archeological remains. We found many pieces of marble from pillars, etc., a large white sarcophagus, and a series of tombs dug in the ground and constructed of rocks. This was great fun — really more exciting than a museum. And tonight we met at the Taverna and ate the fish we had caught.

Nov 12, 1963. Yesterday was a marvelous day, so I left for today the task of writing about it. I spent most of the day just lounging where I am now in a kind of rock throne that is part of a big pile of rocks that juts out into the sea. I sat here and wrote a long letter to Fred, and every once in a while I began to laugh because I could just sit here and have this whole beautiful world all to myself and feel the beautiful sun on my skin and look at the beautiful clear green sea and the sky and the rocky hills and the little white church on the little rocky hill between the two hills to my left and the village with the windmills off in the distance. And the sunset! The sun was perfectly gold as it lowered into the sea, making a shimmering image in the water and coating the entire sea with a gold film. And over on the beach where I went wading with the jellyfish, I wrote this:

Of the Mysteries

I know only as much of God and the world
As a creature with two eyes must;
But what I do understand, I love,
And what I don't understand, I trust.

Then I performed the remarkable feat of shaving my legs in the Mediterranean Sea and I came home.

Nov 13, 1963. There are more clouds than usual in the sky, and I think it is because tonight I must leave Mykonos. Oh, how I do not, not, *not* want to go! As I look out over the white roofs and church crosses and trees and clotheslines and rock walls, I rebel against being jerked back into a world of time and organization.

Nov 18, 1963. Below me and to the left is Mount Olympus. I don't know if any of the old gods still hang out there, but even so I'm closer to heaven than they are. Here I am, on an SAS flight to Vienna, and from there directly to Moscow.

Carol Lynn's ten days in the Soviet Union were a swirl of activities and sightseeing so nonstop that no diarist could have done them justice while they were happening. Carol Lynn made an heroic effort to record as much as she could while on the run, but realizing that she could not both see and write as she would like on that whirlwind trip, she kept notes; afterwards, in the calm environment of her friend Selene's home in Nairobi, she typed fifty pages about her Russian visit. We thought readers might be interested in the difference between a diary kept day-to-day, albeit on the run, and a record composed in detailed form after the fact. So you will first read excerpts from CLW's running diary while she was in Russia, then excerpts from the fifty-page record she wrote a month or so later.

Nov 20, 1963. The lights are dimming in the Vahtangov Theater where I am about to see *Nora* (*A Doll's House*) by Ibsen.

Next day, 7:45: It is intermission at the Bolshoi Ballet, where I am seeing *Giselle,* and it is exquisite. What a gorgeous theater! Six galleries of gold with red plush upholstery. The audience around me looks little different from any other audience; the orchestra tuning up sounds the same as any other; the performance, while marvelous, is not peculiar. The only peculiarity is the small shock I feel whenever I glance at the red star that adorns the top of the proscenium.

Nov 21, 1963. Tonight I went to the services of the Baptist Church here in Moscow and later had a long walk and a long talk with the daughter of the pastor. The episode requires more careful treatment than I have the alertness to give it just now — but one word: some of my illusions are being shattered to slivers. This girl was not lying. I think on many things, she is deceived. But also I think that in many things, I have been deceived. Many.

Nov 22, 1963. I am waiting for breakfast in the Metropole Hotel of Moscow. I cannot even think. It is 9:10 A.M. Moscow time. Ten minutes ago I was informed in the elevator that President John F. Kennedy is dead — assassinated yesterday afternoon in Texas. I cannot even think.

Dec 2, 1963. I am aghast to think how much I have to catch up on, but I must comment on the thing that has occupied my mind more than anything else since it happened. Dozens of times a day I remember that President Kennedy is dead — assassinated! On the morning that I heard it, descending in the elevator, I was speechless. I walked to the cafe in a trance, and saw that the dark-haired waitress whom I had talked to the day before was reading *Pravda* [*a Russian newspaper*]. On the front page was a picture of President Kennedy. She gave me the paper and I sat at the table staring at it. I was crying. As I left, the girl wouldn't take the paper back. "This is for you. I liked President Kennedy. I liked him very much." I could not speak. That morning was my visit to the Moscow Art Theater Acting School, and both the director and the head professor, whom I talked to, expressed their sadness at this terrible thing. And many, many other Russian citizens have told me the same, in sincerity, I know. Back at the hotel, I went up to my room and prayed; and , packing for Leningrad, I sang as loudly as I could, "God Bless America," six or seven times.

Below are some excerpts from the later record, written on January 29, 1964, but covering the November 18-December 3, 1963, period.

I want to try very hard to write as fully as I am able my remembrances of the trip, because certainly it was a remarkable experience, and I want as much as possible to keep time and forgetfulness from robbing it. . . . I will simply classify this as stream-of-consciousness writing.

My mealtimes in Moscow and Leningrad were brightened particularly by one figure whom I think I shall not forget: Mischa Slavensky, a ballet dancer from Australia. He was marvelous. I happened to sit by him at lunch one day, and from that moment we struck up a delightful friendship, and whenever he would see me, he would run over and kiss my hand. About thirty-eight, with completely white hair, a handsome tanned face, and a very good body, he had been born in Yugoslavia, and was now with his partner in Russia as a guest of the government. He wore a fur hat that used to belong to his mother, and I can't forget laughing uproariously as he talked about "dis voman hat." When we would eat together, we would somehow keep infringing on each other's butter. So he would take to slapping my fingers and saying, "My butter; don't touch!" Once we danced together (there were always orchestras around), and it was great fun. "What, Carol, are you rich? I shall marry you straightaway." Charming, charming, charming.

To give a true picture of all the facets of my Russian experience, I guess I must mention another character in Moscow. There was a hockey team from Canada there playing against the Russian team. I talked to the captain of the team a couple of times, a tall blond man whose name I don't remember. Then late one night as I was just getting into bed, my telephone rang — and it was him. He said he wanted to come and talk to me right now. I said I was practically in bed, and it was impossible; I'd talk to him tomorrow. No, it was very important, he said, and he had to see me now. Well, somehow I conjured up the idea that maybe there was a political intrigue going on, and that maybe he was the head of a spy ring or something, so with this faint hope in mind, I told him he could come up for just a minute. No, CLW never learns; she spent too much time reading *Nancy Drew* and *Anne of Green Gables* while other people were reading D. H. Lawrence. Of course this gentleman was not the head of a spy ring. And after a short scene in which I felt some revolting Fate was trying to cast me as The Woman in the hotel scene of *Death of a Salesman*, nylons and all, I got rid of him. I kicked myself all the way to bed for being so dumb.

One episode that highlighted CLW's trip to Russia featured a young man named Vladik. The account of this incident runs to seven single-spaced typed pages, more than we have room for here, but we'd be cheating readers if we left the story out altogether, so here it is, in a highly condensed form:

That was the night I met Vladik. After the ballet finished, we went out front to claim our coats. As I was standing there, a young man spoke to me.

"You must forgive my bad English," he said, "I do not speak good English when I am drunk. And tonight I am a little drunk."

"Oh," I said. "And why are you drunk tonight?"

He shrugged and smiled. "Because I never understand the ballet except when I'm drunk."

He asked if he could see me the next day, and I very quickly examined the idea. This is what I had wanted: an opportunity to visit with somebody strictly off the record and get a different perspective on Soviet life. So I said yes.

At dinner the next day I told the others that I was going somewhere with my friend whom they had seen last night and that they could tell Sophie [*the guide*] anything they cared to, and if she wanted to send the Soviet Police out for me, she could. And for Mr. Griff's peace of mind, I told him that if I wasn't back by midnight, he could call the American Embassy. I collected my coat and hat . . . and casually walked out the revolving door, crossed the street, and joined a young man in a gray felt hat.

"What are you doing in Russia?" asked Vladik as we started walking past St. Isaac's.

"I'm a spy."

"Really?" His joy was unconcealed. Of course, I then had to

disappoint him by admitting that in actual fact I was not a spy and was in his country on the quite mundane status of tourist. I am not going to apologize for the incautious behavior of that day. . . . Everything went along in a very proper way, and I regard the experience as a highly profitable one.

As we stood there on the corner with the ice freezing my feet, Vladik said . . . that he would go and get a bottle of vodka for us. I asked him please not to, as I did not drink vodka or any other kind of alcohol. . . . Well, he had to have some anyway, he said; he had a very bad cold and it was essential that he have some vodka. I told him I was sure that vodka was not the proper thing for a cold. But he said that indeed it was the best thing in the world. And leaving me there on the corner, he dashed off. . . . In a moment he came racing back with a large bottle under his arm. . . . Vladik then was most apologetic, and said that it would just take a few minutes, but that he must make a business call immediately; apparently his entire future career depended on it. . . . We walked about half a block and climbed several flights of dark, ugly stairs. . . . He knocked at a door, and nobody answered. At this, he was quite distraught, and said please would I mind waiting here for just a minute. . . . As there was very little I could do about it, I said I would be positively delighted to wait in that charming murky hallway. "Good," and he shoved the bottle of vodka at me for me to hold, and he leaped down the stairs.

Now, really, this was too ridiculous: me standing alone in my fur coat and hat in a dingy hallway several stories up in a strange apartment building in Leningrad — holding a bottle of *vodka!* I quickly shoved the bottle into my great purse and assumed an air of intense belonging. Whenever anybody would walk up or down the stairs and look at me suspiciously, I exuded belongingness and became one with the peeling wallpaper.

Before too long, happy Vladik came bounding up the stairs and together we walked down the stairs and outside. About a block or so away, we arrived at his apartment house.

His roommate was there, a young, pleasant-looking boy who didn't speak English. The apartment was very small and scantily furnished.

Vladik told me he was planning to escape from his country as some of his friends had done, through Finland. . . . Vladik described to me how they would do it, and in great glee had his fingers run across the couch in a superb get-away.

111

I asked Vladik if he believed in God. He didn't know.

"Once, when the police were chasing me, I was very frightened, and I prayed very hard that the police would not find me. They did not find me. And so I think that maybe there is a God."

I told him that I knew there was a God, and that not always would there be such difficulties in the world. I remembered that I had one Church pamphlet left in my purse, so I gave it to him and made him promise to read it — *The Plan of Salvation*.

During the visit in Vladik's apartment, their discussion ranged over subjects such as Russian plays and films, Russian girls, politics, and related topics.

As it was almost getting dark, I insisted on going, although Vladik was very anxious not to have me leave. But he was gentlemanly about it. And, of course, he came with me; in fact, his roommate did, too. As we walked to catch the trolley, the sky was becoming dark, and lights of the city were beginning to go on. And of course it was cold. I walked between the two Russian boys and put both my arms through theirs. And I thought — about Russians and Americans and Moscow and Leningrad and New York City and Provo and God and Atheism and nuclear rockets and newspapers and snow and Christians and President Kennedy and Mr. Kruschev — and people, as people.

At the trolley stop, the roommate left us, and I told him goodbye and that I would see him in heaven. [*On the trolley*] Vladik started telling me what a wonderful, nice, pretty, good girl I was.

"You are the best girl I have ever met. Oh, Carol, why you not stay in Leningrad and marry with me?"

Well, thank goodness trolley rides don't last forever. By the time we got to the hotel, he was quite sure that he was very much in love with me. . . .

The next morning when I went into the lounge, Vladik was sitting there uncomfortably talking to an American tourist who had cornered him. So for about forty-five minutes we sat there, neither one of us feeling very jolly. I don't remember a thing we talked about. . . . The next day I sent him one of my New Year's cards from Kiev, telling him I would think of him and hope he had a very good 1964. Before long, his black market business will be picking up, with the tourist season getting better. Or perhaps by now he has been arrested again and is in prison — or perhaps shot, whatever they do to perpetual offenders. I think I will pretend that he has escaped to Finland.

Dec 6, 1963. I'll never get caught up, never. What a marvelous place I am in: I am in heaven. . . . I am in my room in the St. George Hotel in Jerusalem. I can't believe it — Jerusalem!

Saturday, Dec 7, 1963. Oh, Bethlehem was better in my dreams!

I sit here on the bus waiting to go back to Jerusalem. Out the window I can see a few yellowish houses, and a few green trees on the rocky hillside. And to my left are children with play rifles and men with long gray shirts and white head coverings. Down underneath is the place where supposedly Christ was actually born. I guess I didn't really expect to walk in and smell hay and hear lambs bleating, but I would have much preferred that to the smell of perfumed wax and the sound of Latin chanting that I met. Anyway, I was not impressed. However, my somewhat disappointing experience found a compensation. As the bus began to move, I looked to my left, and there against the graying sky was a silhouette of houses on the hillside. And above, really and truly, was one bright star, the only one in the sky. I smiled and smelled the hay and heard the lambs bleat.

Dec 10, 1963. I went first to the Garden Tomb — a beautiful place with flowers and trees and birds and a white tomb with an opening and an interior where one can easily imagine the body of Christ having been laid. I sat outside the tomb for a while and read the account of the resurrection.

Dec 11, 1963. Just after noon today, the plane landed in Nairobi — and there were no rhinos or tribal chiefs to greet me; but in a minute, in rushed lovely Selene carrying her lovely baby. Of course, I was ecstatic to see them both.

Dec 28, 1963. There are a number of things that can blight my life, certain among them being: having been slothful about praying, having dirty hair, and being behind in my diary.

Jan 1, 1964. *New Year's Day on the River Nile.* At present the sun is behind a cloud, giving us relief from the tropical heat. What a marvelous trip! Close enough almost to touch them: crocodile, elephants, hippopotamus. We've seen hundreds of each today. I went to the back and sat where one of the black boys was dragging his feet in the water. Green banks, fluffy clouds, lily pads, French people in boats, flocks of birds in patterned flight, a stray heron — beautiful and exciting.

Jan 22, 1964. Letter from Fred. I cannot imagine — in all the realms of possibility — how it is I can go on caring so much about him — no matter what the circumstances.

Feb 10, 1964. This morning we went shopping, and I bought two cheap pens, one expensive drum, and one valentine. My drum is a little uneven on the bottom, but it has the most beautiful skin I've ever seen on a drum (zebra skin), and though it cost $10 — now a fortune to my rapidly diminishing funds — I got it.

Feb 12, 1964. This morning three ladies came over to pay a social visit in good embassy tradition. They were very nice ladies, and the conversation was very nice, and I would go mad if I had to do that very often.

Feb 15, 1964. What a gorgeous thing it is to watch giraffe loping along the African landscape. And impala and gazelle gliding along, and leaping, and zebra standing close, stripes running together, and ostriches running ungainly across the road, and a golden thorn tree against the setting African sun. Loved it. We drove today to the Masai game preserve bordering on Tanganyika.

Feb 16, 1964. I spent some time out in the sun this morning, reading some pamphlets the Israeli Embassy sent me — one on the kibbutz and another on the Hebrew Theater. Did I mention that I am arranging to live on a kibbutz for a few weeks while I stop off in Israel on my way home? I am quite excited about it.

Mar 3, 1964. We have another Askari now. During Uhuru, the embassy gave everybody one, but now that the crime wave has gone up one-third, they're assigning them again. What does an Askari do? He wears a purple fez and stands guard outside *all night long* so that no one bothers the house. And I don't much care to think about someone outside my window holding a panga [*large knife*]. Just this second he coughed, and it gives me the creeps.

Mar 9, 1964. I can't imagine why Fred wants us to keep on writing; am I just a very interesting pen-pal? But even as I write this I know I'm not writing the real truth. There is so much more. And this business is not "absurd." There is some logic behind it all that I cannot even begin to penetrate. And when I try to understand it, I only end up in tears. And it frightens me and exhausts me and angers me that I must go on living with something I do not understand.

Mar 18, 1964. Well, tonight is my last night on the soil of Kenya. I'm flying out tomorrow at 1 A.M.

Mar 24, 1964. This kibbutz has three hundred people in it (not counting foreigners and apprentices like me). There will be three classes. We eat in a large dining room, grabbing whatever we want. Yesterday morning I worked mending a mattress and ironing upholstery covers. Also that morning I received my work clothes — two shirts and two pair of pants and socks. Yesterday afternoon I went wandering around the farm. It's quite decent-looking but smells a bit farmy. Just below is a lovely valley with trees members here planted many years ago. I walked down to them and sat a while and thought.

Mar 28, 1964. In our room is a large stack of unleavened bread, for we are now in the season of the Passover. Yesterday was the beginning. At 4:30 in the afternoon, there was a ceremony with singing and dancing in one of the near fields. A narrator told about the exodus, tying it into the kibbutz, I believe. Later we went to the large theater and ate and watched the program. One song told of Moses bringing water with his stick. ("Miem," the audience would respond.) Another told of the journey through the Red Sea. For one part, we all stood in the dark while someone read a poem to commemorate the deaths of those who died defending modern Israel and in the concentration camps. Afterwards, Jim (from Portland and Harvard) and I almost went to a dance in the dining room. I say "almost" because there were people and no music, so we came home.

Mar 30, 1964. Also last night I wrote a letter to Fred. Always when I finish writing a letter to Fred, I look around me almost startled and say, "Where am I?"

Apr 12, 1964. "They shall also make gardens and eat the fruit of them." (Amos.) This is what I've been doing every morning for the last week, working in the gardens of the gathered children of Israel. I think to myself that it's sort of an exciting thing to participate in this, but when the day is cold and wet and rainy as it was today, then even this small satisfaction doesn't help me. Last Sunday I dug gladiolus bulbs, and since then I have picked oranges, painted small grapefruit trees, and thinned peach buds.

The language! What a frustrating thing it is to be unable to read a simple sentence — entirely new letters, no vowels, and with a backward order. There are about sixteen in our class. Our teacher Rotha speaks only in Hebrew (with a little English thrown in), so it requires strenuous concentration!

Apr 22, 1964. How busy I am! I have no time to do anything I want —

like keep up this diary. Picking oranges, working in the kitchen, and today, ironing twenty-six shirts. And classes all afternoon. Last night I went to a play in the theater here.

May 9, 1964. How silly to spend two hours playing Scrabble — in *Hebrew!*

May 13, 1964. I've been peeling onions and cutting carrots and cleaning chicken gizzards and all manner of fun things.

May 18, 1964. Last Wednesday, Jim and I walked to the theater and back again and watched the army games — all the soldiers spent a week at a camp just next door to our place, shooting flares, bullet tracers, all kinds of fun things. Needless to say, the observation of this dress rehearsal, seven and a half miles from Armageddon was an absorbing experience.

Early Friday morning, I set out for Jerusalem.

I went to the Notre Dame dorm-hostel, but learned that their rooms were not open, and a regular room cost six lire ($2) per night — out of my price range. So the gardener told me that the *hospital* next door sometimes gives rooms to people who have no place to stay. So he took me over, and the white-clad little French nuns conferenced and decided to take me in. So one led me to an unused ward of ten beds and directed me to one. How weird — sleeping in an empty hospital ward in a French hospital in Jerusalem! But I deposited my things and went out to see the city.

On the roof of the Notre Dame building was a tired-looking lady from Hungary, walking her dog, and I talked with her for a bit. From there, I walked down to the Mendelbaum Gate. A young man was singing a prayer, and after, I saw him again and spoke to him. We talked for half an hour. Later, eating my bread and butter and orange, I was accosted by a group of young boys, maybe twelve of them, who talked to me a bit in Hebrew. Walking back into town, I talked with American tourists.

In front of the Hebrew Union College building, I met Curly: short, bearded (of course), from Brooklyn, and with a true gentlemanly heart. He had also been at Ein Hashofet on an Ulpan, and was now attending the university. After we talked for a while, he invited me down to the kitchen for goodies. Sunday morning, Curly, his friend Victor, and I met for synagogue service at 10 A.M. at the Union College. We were just

116

on time, but the place was full, and we had to stand (many people couldn't even enter).

May 27, 1964. (back at the kibbutz). I think it will be a good thing for me when Jim leaves. I am too much aware of him daily.

I worked eight hours today: four ironing in the children's house and four scrubbing in the music room. (Every two weeks we put in a full day's work instead of classes.) Tired!

Jun 22, 1964. So I am leaving the old Zion to go home to the new. I am leaving the gathering of Judah to join the gathering of Israel.

Fred is engaged to be married.

Jul 14, 1964. Already we are flying over the North American continent, and in about half an hour, will land in New York. We stopped briefly in Lisbon, Portugal.

America. What is this land to which I am returning? I've come to realize that America is not the land of utter perfection that I guess I thought it was somewhere in my uninformed dreams. The land of America is just part of the soil of the earth. And the people of America are just part of the people of the earth. But somehow, this land and this people — perhaps through a virtue of their own, perhaps not — have been given a part to play in this world that is remarkable. I was born to America, and I was born to a part of America that has a unique destiny. I am part of that destiny. There is no fulfillment for me apart from it. And it is there that I am going.

Jul 16, 1964. I write from a booth just outside the Mormon Pavilion at the World's Fair. What a marvelous way to be welcomed back to America! The exhibit is very nicely done, with dozens of eager, fresh young missionaries standing about and explaining various parts of the exhibit. The tabernacle organ plays and I watch people stream out of the pavilion past a picture that I stared at on my bed in Israel, the colored picture of Joseph Smith that reads, "Joseph Smith's Testimony." What a thrill all this is!

My mother was on a mission in the Eastern States. I'm sure she never imagined the sight I'm seeing today.

Jul 20, 1964. Many things to write, but one won't wait. What an unbelievable thing happened yesterday — one of those things that Fate must have planned carefully for a long time: I ran into Fred and his wife on their honeymoon.

117

I went to church in the Manhattan Ward, and just as we were dismissing for Sunday School, I saw him. In the course of saying hello, I asked if he were married, as I sensed that he didn't know how to tell me. "Yes," he said, and introduced me to his wife: short, pretty, with red hair and a yellow dress. After church, we talked again just a minute, and I gave them wedding congratulations and best wishes for the future.

The end of a book. The end of an era. I don't have a new book. I don't have a new era. It will take me a little while to get both. But I shall.

"Sometime I will write some really good things"

By the week of August 21, 1964, Carol Lynn was safely back in Provo, but elsewhere in the world, danger was brewing. Newspapers recorded the first direct United States action against North Vietnam – an air strike ordered by President Lyndon Johnson after torpedo boats twice attacked a United States destroyer in the Gulf of Tonkin. Controversy over America's role in the Vietnam conflict would eventually become violent and bitter, forming the central issue of student riots on college campuses during the late sixties. The Brigham Young University campus remained calm throughout the decade, with students who were not only peaceful and law-abiding but well-groomed, following the policies set forth by the university's Board of Trustees. Elsewhere, male college students grew shoulder-length hair and chest-length beards, and both men and women adopted a deliberately casual, often careless, style of dress. Back at BYU, Carol Lynn began a third career: she had been student and actress for five years, teacher for one, and now she was to devote herself to writing more fully than she had ever done before.

Aug 21, 1964. Two weeks ago at this very hour I was arriving in Provo after having been gone for one year. And here I sit on the front porch of our old house on the corner, not wanting to write up a month in one entry. Checking now, I see that my last diary ended on July 20. *One extraordinarily bad paragraph of pieces:*

In New York: Jeani and Neil were marvelous — likewise their air-conditioned apartment. *Richard III* at Stratford, Connecticut — great. Tabernacle Choir at World's Fair. World's Fair not such a big deal

119

after you've seen the world itself. *High Spirits* with Bea Lillie and Tammy Grimes — didn't like it; all personalities and no play. *Othello* in Central Park — good. *Three Sisters* at Actor's Studio — terribly depressing for no reason. Race riots all through New York. Cumorah Pageant, Dr. Hansen. Provo. Have accomplished little. Visited with people — Dave J., Selene (arrived home the very day I did), Joan and Dave, Helen and LaVar and Aunt Mamie, Marie in Salt Lake, Margy Potter in Salt Lake. Typed my poems from my diaries. Organized a few of my things. Wrote letters. Had a date last night. Large waste of time, both the activity and the person.

This style of diary-keeping obviously is not Carol Lynn's usual one, but notice that it does effectively wrap up a large block of time in a relatively short space. Sometimes even a "list entry" – just a jotting down in one-two-three order of the whats, the wheres, and the whos – can be valuable and appropriate. Don't let yourself get bogged down because of a feeling that you must write a full page of full sentences every time you open your journal. Be receptive to different ways of keeping your journal.

Aug 25, 1964. Homeless in my own home town. Whoever thought that I'd be looking for an apartment in Provo? Well, I now have one and will move in soon — with Margy and another girl. And it was quite a task. But it's a nice place.

CLW's father and stepmother were serving a mission at this time, and the family home was rented to some relatives.

Aug 31, 1964. Last week Dave J. made an appointment for me to see Scott Whitaker of the BYU Motion Picture Department. He had read some of my things and thought I could perhaps do some writing for them.

Now about Larry. Dear Larry — dear eternal, everlasting Larry. Yesterday Dave J. decided to go up to Ogden . . . so suddenly I decided to go up with him. I went to Larry's apartment, and as there was a note to T. telling him to go in and make himself at home, I did. In about an hour, Larry came . . . Marvelous visit for several hours. Without any hesitancy, we tumbled back into the very, very close and good relationship that has characterized the best of Magnolia and Jazbo. He's going to California . . . as he has a teaching job there that pays him lots more than in Ogden, and also helps him in taking classes to finish his master's. I'm glad he has this thing to go to. But I hate, hate, hate to see him leave. . . . I like to think he's somewhere near.

Sep 6, 1964. This morning I spoke to the Relief Society at the campus ward where LaVar is bishop. I spoke on Israel, and they all seemed to quite enjoy it.

Didn't mention that last night I sang my Hebrew song at a stake party up at the Girls' Home. I've never before sung alone in public, and it was great fun.

Sep 10, 1964. I have just finished reading again my one-act play, *Holders of the Mirror*, with the thought in mind of sending it to Jim.

Most of Tuesday I spent writing another script for the BYU Motion Picture people.

Yesterday I studied a lot of Hebrew. And I received a very nice letter from LeGrand Richards. I had sent to him the article on Israel I wrote for the *Era*.

CLW then copies out the letter from Elder Richards; this correspondence is the result of an August 25 meeting between Elder Richards and CLW.

Sep 17, 1964. Tonight I had to help at a "Meet Your Bishop" night — group fun and games. Don C. again brought me home (as from an MIA party some weeks ago). I liked him better the first time. I'm deciding again that I don't want to spend time with boys unless they're remarkable.

Sep 20, 1964. Men for dinner. (Not on the table — around it.) Two men from down the street. Earl — whom Margy has dated off and on for quite a while — and Tim R., whom I happen to think is very interesting indeed.

Sep 22, 1964. One nice thing of today: B. Davis Evans of Spanish Fork High told me he wants to produce *Pegora* and offered $40 royalty.

Oct 3, 1964. Both Thursday and Friday classes [*CLW is teaching part-time at BYU*] went really well. I do enjoy the in-class time. But I'd rather write ten themes than read and grade ten.

Oct 6, 1964. Last night I spoke on Israel to the Ninth Ward Special Interest group. It went well.

Today Scott Whitaker called me and asked if I could help a little on a rush filmstrip they're doing on the family home evening program the Church pushed at conference.

Oct 8, 1964. 2:50 P.M. I sit on my lovely sheepskin from Greece and listen to my lovely Judy Garland record in my own lovely apartment. This is good. This is good.

An extra in the BYU movie And Should We Die

Scott Whitaker came by an hour ago to pick up a poem they asked me to write especially for a filmstrip they're doing for the World's Fair.

Oct 10, 1964. "Judge" (W. O.) Whitaker called me yesterday and wanted me to come down to see him. He told me how very impressed he was with my work for them, and how he wants me to do more. On projects all my own (like the open-end thing) I'll sell them straight across. But on rewrites and just helping out — what would I work for? I told him I felt my time for them should be at least as valuable as the time I spent correcting freshman themes — so we agreed on $2.75 per hour. I guess that's fair enough. He gave me a commercial filmstrip to work on — selling land in California. I guess it's a start. Also, Scott gave me the whole World's Fair filmstrip to re-touch.

The exciting thing is that this will enable me to sometime write some really good things for the Church.

Since that time, Carol Lynn has indeed written some "really good things" for the BYU Motion Picture Studio and for the Church. She had worked on countless filmstrips and films, but the script that has had perhaps the widest acclaim and circulation is the one she wrote for Cipher in the Snow, *a production that has won awards and heartfelt acceptance not only in the Church but far beyond.*

Oct 13, 1964. Sunday evening, I spoke at the fireside of our ward — on Israel. It went well. And this evening I spoke on the same thing at Dave's ward up in the Y Center.

Something happened in Church Sunday evening that I want to forget. Just as the sacrament started, Darla made a hilarious comment to me that just cracked me right up. I was chortling under my breath, biting my lip and *dying* for a full twenty minutes. Nothing like this has happened to me since I was in grade school. I couldn't believe it.

Oct 16, 1964. Tim came over for a little while tonight. He is a rat. But I like him better all the time. The rat.

As I sit here, I have written a little item that I don't understand, but at the moment I like it.

> If you see me
> Ankle-deep in the stream
> Just above where it turns
> To a great waterfall,

> Shaking a little
> Perhaps because of the chill,
> Holding to my lips
> A dripping stone,
>
> Keep silent.

This very moment he [*Tim*] is playing music through the wall a few feet away. He tapped at me and I tapped back.

The rat.

Oct 25, 1964. To live in this world requires a huge and consistent self-trust and self-confidence — a huge self-approval. I do not have this — at least not consistently. This devil discouragement is thriving in my life. And I must exorcise it. But I am not strong.

Tonight I spoke at the fireside of the Ninth Ward Young Marrieds. Brother Warren and Diane were there.

Nov 13, 1964. Friday. Well: I am now in a play. There are reasons why I shouldn't be — but I can't help myself. It's been about sixteen months since I last was in a play — and that's too long. The play is Thornton Wilder's *The Skin of Our Teeth*. I've always loved the play . . . [*Director Charles Metten*] didn't assign parts, but he read me a lot for Mrs. Antrobus. I'd dearly love to do Sabina, but I guess you have to be innately sexy for that one.

An exciting thing: a letter from Walter Wager, editor of *Playbill*:

Dear Miss Wright—

I have read and re-read your article about your visit to the Moscow Art Theater School. I am currently considering it very seriously for our February issue, which will be devoted to the theater in the Soviet Union. . . .

> Sincerely,
> Walter Wager

Nov 20, 1964. I got a letter from the *Relief Society Magazine* saying they want to use my sonnet — "Joseph's Gift." But I think I want to rewrite it first.

Last Saturday I bought a hairdryer, which I love. And a pair of black leather stacked-heel calf-high boots. They're all the rage now, and wonderfully warm. And Wednesday I bought a carrying case after all these years of lugging stacks of books and papers around. I have no money. How can I buy things?

Nov 26, 1964. There is a tremendous impatience in my stomach. There is so much I want to do. And so little time to do it. Why do we have to have bodies to feed and clothe and put to bed and fret over? Just to keep us humble, I guess.

Dec 5, 1964. A nice thing happened today: I got a letter from Edward Grusd, saying he wants to publish my article on the Jovail Dancers in the *National Jewish Monthly*. This makes me very happy indeed. He didn't mention anything about payment — but the important thing is that Jews all over America will read about the LDS Church in terms of the Jovail Dancers — and from *me*. This is exciting.

Dec 12, 1964. Tonight Dave and I went to see the BYU Folkdancers at the fieldhouse. They were great — great — great. And I was tremendously excited at having *my* school do something so good. I want BYU to be the best of everything in the entire world. There's so much to be done. I almost burst to think how much there is to be done. And I must be content to do only tiny, tiny things. But I *will* do things — however tiny.

Dec 29, 1964. Last week I was low one day. I went over to the press to pick up my scripts of *Pegora* that I had bound. The lady at the desk (whom I didn't know) said, "Whenever I see you, I think of Joan of Arc. I've never seen anything so beautiful as that. And my two children sat enraptured."

The entire texture of my day was changed.

Jan 6, 1965. Joy — delight — wonder — ecstasy! Thrilling day!

At 1 P.M. I ran into my office panting and answered the phone. The operator asked for me. Then a male voice said:

"Hello. This is Walter Wager of *Playbill* in New York."

Me: (grasping at the desk): Sir — I'm delighted to hear from you.

Him: How are you, Miss Wright?

Me: Very well, thank you. And you?

Him: I'm young, charming, and handsome.

Me: Wonderful!

Him: But that's not what I called about. I'm sending you a check. We're going to publish your article.

Me: (Gasp, choke, inane statement.)

Him: I had quite a battle with the other editor about it, but finally truth and beauty prevailed and we're going to use it.

He went on to ask some biographical facts and such. . . .

125

I exploded! I absolutely lost my head in ecstasy. I ran up and down the room hopping and shaking. I couldn't work, of course.

Jan 9, 1965. Thursday I received a letter from Mr. Wager of *Playbill* saying I would receive a check for $150. Marvelous!

Yesterday I mailed off nineteen copies of *Pegora* to various people who do children's theater. I included stamped return envelopes, and it cost me a goodly sum — $8 — so I hope something comes of it.

Jan 21, 1965. What charming mail I'm getting these days! Today arrived a check from the *National Jewish Monthly* — for $75. Lovely — lovely.

Corrected themes all day long.

Jan 23, 1965. Through, I am through. Yesterday, I handed in grades. How I hate to grade. Hate it. How can I trust my own omniscience to be just? I hate it.

Feb 11, 1965. Rehearsals have been going well. Tonight was good. Last night was rotten. I enjoy rehearsals. Dr. Metten is very good indeed. And I get on well with all the other actors.

It's interesting how I've changed since my freshman days. I have no insecurities about my abilities as an actress (this point never really worried me), but more important, I have no doubt about my abilities to measure up as a person — which has been my A number-one problem. I haven't played aloof because of my faculty-staff status or my past glories. And I'm buddies with a lot of the kids. This I like. And they like me.

Today I sent off a poetry book manuscript to the Utah State Poetry Society contest. I typed up fifty pages of my best poems, and I even gave the collection a name: *Magnolias on a Thorn Tree.*

Feb 19, 1965. The second night of the play is over. It has gone very well both nights. It's really a very polished production, I think.

I like my part, but it won't be *the* favorite thing I've ever done when I come to the end of my life.

I haven't mentioned the cast, have I? Dan Staples, my husband, a young man of outstanding ability. Sabina — Michelle Pribe — does very well. Gladys — Stephanie Nielsen — is good, and Henry also — thirty-year-old Glen Varney.

The third act is hard. And the audience can't get the idea that it's serious.

Oh, one other person in the play I must mention: Gerald Pearson. He's a twenty-two-year-old returned missionary, and we have struck up a marvelous little friendship. He has beautiful blond hair and is completely open and unfeigning. I like him. And he likes me — he really does. He thinks I'm "terribly witty and a fantastic actress" and that I have "beautiful bright expressive eyes that shine from deep, deep down."

If I didn't know better, I might develop a crush on him. Maybe I will anyway.

Postscript

If the foregoing chapters have stirred your interest in journal-keeping (and we hope they have!), you may be interested in a few final suggestions.

First, if you've enjoyed dipping into someone else's diaries, perhaps you'd like to read more. Two good books will help get you started. *A Treasury of the World's Great Diaries*, edited by Dunaway and Evans (Doubleday, 1957), contains brief excerpts from some of the most interesting diaries of the past three centuries — usually about eight or ten pages from each one. Included are the writings of Davy Crockett and Anne Frank, Mark Twain and Queen Victoria, the great actor John Barrymore and a marvelously precocious little girl of six named Marjory Fleming, Louisa May Alcott and a survivor of the bombing of Hiroshima — and many more. If you find in this fine anthology a person whose journal especially interests you, you can then go to a library and look up the complete published diary to pursue in depth. Then, more nearly in our own backyard, you might want to glance through the *Guide to Mormon Diaries and Autobiographies* by Davis Bitton (Brigham Young University Press, 1977). Many of these journals have not been published; copies of the original handwritten version are available on microfilm. In some cases, the journals have been typed or mimeographed from the originals. The *Guide* tells in which library — BYU, University of Utah, Church Historical Society, and so on — the diaries can be found. You might even find the writings of one of your own ancestors listed. In any case, it's worth a look.

Finally, here are some very specific ideas we've used in the past to suggest what kind of things would-be journal-keepers could include in their records. Look them over and see if any of them start your mental wheels turning:

1. *Who are you? How do you see yourself?* Take a pencil and sheet of paper, and as quickly as you can, write down fifteen *one-word* completions for this sentence: "I am a _____." Don't describe yourself; just write down nouns that you think fit you. Even if it's hard to think of fifteen, push yourself. Don't get help from anyone. Then, when you're done, analyze the results. Is there a pattern? Do you see yourself as a doer: "I am a swimmer .... an artist ... a student"? Do you see yourself basically in relationship to other people: "I am a daugh-

ter... a friend... a brother"? What else do you learn from your answers? Copy the list in your journal, with the date and your age. Repeat the exercise a year from now, or several years from now. Compare lists. See how you change, and in what direction.

2. *Describe one aspect of your life.* How interesting and illuminating it is to read journals and letters from one hundred years ago, when the writers give us good, rich detail about the little things in their lives — aspects that are often so different from ours! Your school day may seem very ordinary to you, but it will be fascinating to your posterity. Describe one school day from start to finish: What time did you get up? What duties did you have around home? What did you wear? How many students were in your school? What classes were you taking and what did you do that particular day in each class? What did you have for lunch? What extracurricular activities did you take part in? What kind of things were your friends talking about and interested in that day? What songs were playing on the car radio? Paint a vivid word-picture that will glow brightly for years to come.

3. *Look at yourself and your family.* Record some impressions and attitudes about your family and its activities. You might start by answering questions like these: How am I most like my mother or father? How am I least like them? How is my family different from the other families I know? What goals are really important to us as a family?

4. *Write some poems* and include them in your journal. Then read some good poems, and write some more. Make notes about which poems you like, and jot *those* down in your journal.

5. *Trace your progress* concerning attainment of one specific goal for three months or six months. Save four or five pages in your journal, and keep a log of your development in one area of your life. This could deal with any aspect: maybe you are learning to ski — keep a record of your outings, your accomplishments, your feelings about skiing from the very first day of instruction. Maybe, on the other hand, you are trying hard to develop patience. Keep an account of your battle with impatience, and what method you try — account for your victories and your losses. Or perhaps you have been chosen for the a cappella choir. Keep an account of all you do and feel about this activity for one semester. Record titles of songs you learn, dates and details of performances, friends you make in the group, and especially your feelings and thoughts.

6. *Draw up a roster* of "People I Like to Keep an Eye On." In your journal, list the following categories:
   a. My own age
   b. Young adult (unmarried)
   c. Young married woman or man
   d. Mature woman or man
Now, from the people you know personally, pick out one person whom you admire and would like to emulate. Do this for each of the four categories. Describe that person. Explain your relationship. Point out what you admire. It would even be fun to talk with some of them and ask specific questions about how they achieved whatever it is that you admire. Record their answers. You'll find it fascinating to check back later in your life and see how closely you came to matching (or surpassing) their examples.

7. *Record your testimony.* Testimonies are personal, growing things. Your testimony changes from year to year, and, of course, your testimony is unique. No one else has a witness exactly like yours. Write out your testimony, being specific and personal, and save it in your journal so that you can re-read it and share it with others as years go by. Some people like to do this each year during their birthday week.

Here are some additional topics to think about:

8. *Personal responses to the scriptures you are reading.* Does a particular passage hit home? Why? Do you have questions? What are they? Can you do as Nephi says, and "liken the scriptures unto yourselves"?

9. *Faith-promoting stories.* The closer to home the better. One ox amazingly lifted out of the mire in Orem — and witnessed by *you* — is more moving as far as individual testimony is concerned than ten Red Seas parted in Egypt.

10. *Signs of the times.* Fulfillment of prophecies could fill many journals. Be alert to the world around you and the way in which the Lord is achieving his purposes.

11. *Major events in the Church.* No time in history has been as momentous as ours. As temples are built, new areas opened to the gospel, new programs implemented, and so forth, record the news and your feelings about it all.

12. *Your spiritual goals.* Where do you hope to be, in your spiritual progress, at age twenty-five? at thirty? at fifty? How do you plan to get there?

13. *Record anything "virtuous, lovely, or of good report, or praiseworthy."*